Beg, Borrow, Steal

Also by Michael Greenberg

Hurry Down Sunshine

Beg, Borrow, Steal

A Writer's Life

Michael Greenberg

Other Press
New York

The stories in this book appeared, in an. earlier form,
in the author's Freelance column in the *Times Literary
Supplement* between June 2003 and April 2009.

Production Editor: Yvonne E. Cárdenas

Book design: Carin Goldberg

This book was set in Garamond 3 and Monospace 821 by
Alpha Design & Composition of Pittsfield, NH.

10 9 8 7 6 5 4 3 2 1

Library of Congress Cataloging-in-Publication Data

Greenberg, Michael, 1952–
  Beg, borrow, steal : a writer's life / Michael Greenberg.
    p. cm.
  ISBN 978-1-59051-341-5 (hardcover) — ISBN 978-1-59051-
358-3 (e-book)
  1. Greenberg, Michael, 1952– 2. Journalists—United States—
Biography. I. Title.
  PN4874.G6775A3 2009
  070.92—dc22
  [B]

2009017790

To Pat Cremins

and to my friend and editor James Campbell

Table of Contents

Beg, Borrow, Steal

Brotherly Love

MY OLD MAN was like Zeus's father Cronos: he couldn't bear the idea that any of his children might surpass him. Life radiated from the central pulse of his scrap-metal yard; the world beyond it seemed to make him defensive and nervous. Self-conscious about his lack of formal education, he took my bookishness as a personal affront. "Which do you think is worth more," he once asked me, "a commodity or some goddamn idea?"

Among the family, my violent fights with him were famous. The last one occurred when I was fifteen. I followed him around the apartment, taunting him with a line from my latest poem, "Which do you think is worth more, flesh or steel?" At the end of his rope, he took a wild swing at me. I dodged it easily, hearing the crush of bone as his fist hit the wall. I fled the apartment, and when I returned, three days later, his hand was in a cast. "You have guts, but no common sense," he said. "One cancels out the other. A total waste."

A week later, I moved away from home, supporting myself with a night job in a bookstore.

Nevertheless, when I was in my early twenties, driving a cab, with a newborn son at home, my father offered me a chance to join the family business. "You get all the major holidays," he said. "You quit work every day at five. And to make a living you don't have to be a genius."

He seemed hurt when I turned him down. "Those notebooks you scribble in won't get you on the goddamn subway," he said.

He was right, and during the lean years that followed I sometimes imagined that he was eyeing me with satisfaction. I was getting what I deserved. The idea of writing for a living was ludicrous to him, unless you were as famous as Arthur Miller or cooked up gags for one of his revered television stars. My literary ambitions were self-destructive and pretentious.

The family metal business was not pretentious. Pig iron, scrap metal, and cold roll steel were the deities of our household. They represented value stripped down to its zero point, tangible and unadorned. To get by in my father's world, you had to be tough, like he was. He didn't have colleagues, only enemies. Every dollar, he taught us, had to be pried away from men who would just as soon see us starve.

My brothers, Robert and Ben, had accepted his offer to join the business, and when he died, nine years ago, they inherited it. More than a livelihood, it had become the source of our family's identity, our New York achievement. Our immigrant grandfather had started with scrap metal back in the 1920s. Prior to that, in the Ukraine, iron work had been the family trade. Robert and Ben enjoyed a special status for keeping this tradition (and, by extension, our Jewish forefathers) alive.

I am stunned, therefore, when I learn that my brothers have decided to liquidate the business and retire while still in their prime. The news puts me in the untenable position of mourning the passing of something that I had strongly rejected.

I ride the number 6 train to the South Bronx in order to see the place one last time. When I arrive, the cinder-block warehouse is almost empty. "You're looking at a carcass," says Ben, reading my mind. The building has already been sold, he tells me. In a month the new owners will move in, a sprinkler company that used to be down in TriBeCa. Robert examines the remaining scraps of steel, doing his best to look busy. They seem embarrassed by the state of affairs, and uneasy about my being there for no apparent reason other than to scrutinize their lives. "What will you do now?" I ask. "Learn to cook," says Ben sarcastically. "Climb mountains," says Robert. A rat hurries along the warehouse wall. I am reminded of Freud's remark that when rats appear in a dream, they usually stand for the dreamer's siblings.

Sitting with them in their cramped, dusty office, I feel the presence of our father. His larger office was in the adjoining room. It looks much as he left it, except for the addition of an exercise bike that my brothers rarely use. Robert once had aspirations to be an artist, and on the wall opposite our father's old desk hangs a painting he did of the warehouse crammed with rolled coils of steel. The picture of prosperity. "I feel that I'm letting Dad down," says Robert quietly. "He never would have allowed this to happen."

Our father's stamp on him was enormous. A few weeks after our father died, Robert started wearing his pinkie ring, a blue sapphire set in a square of gold. He took to smoking his cigars, driving his old, wheezy Mercedes, and thrusting his chin out like our father, growling at people without provocation. I thought of Patricia Highsmith's character Tom Ripley assuming the mannerisms of his victim Dickie Greenleaf in *The Talented Mr. Ripley*, though in Robert's case this was a benign, seemingly unconscious homage.

A couple of months later, as if snapping out of a trance, he ditched the Mercedes, put away the pinkie ring, and returned to himself—solitary and shy. I realized then that this had been Robert's way of mourning: he had been keeping our father alive in himself.

Ben has few misgivings about quitting. Liquidation, in fact, was his idea. "When I feel guilty," he says, "I remember what I went through with the old man. And I think, to hell with it, I had enough. I can't stand this place anymore." As the eldest son, Ben felt coerced into joining the business. Expectations for him were higher than for the rest of us. Had the pressure been less, he believes, he might have led a more rewarding life doing something else. Our father punished him for that ambivalence. "He'd come in and slap his cane on my desk, spoiling for a fight. 'So you want to get out of here?' he'd ask. Everything I did was wrong." For thirty years they tormented each other with accumulated rancor.

We go to a diner for lunch and return to the office. The afternoon drags slowly on. The phone is silent. The truck awaits a buyer. The line cutter, which was used to shear rolls of steel into sheets like plywood, will soon be hauled to Mexico, where metalwork is thriving. My brothers worry about getting paid. The business has always been small, with rarely more than six employees. Two remain, hanging around with nothing to do, impatient to go home. They remember our father differently than we do. "We called him The Pigeon," says one, "because every time the cutter went silent he'd stick his head out the office window to see what was going on." One morning, eager to get to work, he jumped out of his car while it was still in gear. "It smashed into a fire hydrant, but your father didn't notice. Or he didn't give a damn. He wasn't easy to work for, but that man had drive." The drive kept the business going. My brothers, they believe, have broken a tacit contract. "There just wasn't enough hustle in them. Together they couldn't do what your old man did alone."

I step outside for some air. The last time I was here, in the 1980s, barefoot crack whores prowled the streets in the freezing cold. Today, the neighborhood is slightly less dramatic, though ample signs of misery remain. Flanked by two enormous waste-burning plants, men in rags lower traps into the East River. One snares a blue claw crab. The man next to him looks on jealously. Squatter camps made of discarded car parts spill out from under the expressway.

Shortly before he died, my father recalled the day I turned down his offer to join the business. "It was just as well," he said. "You wouldn't have lasted. Your brothers do better."

Kettle of Fish

WHEN I WAS fifteen, my parents moved from an outer borough of New York to Manhattan. I managed to place myself in a Greenwich Village high school where most of my classmates were "Red Diaper babies," the children of blacklisted leftists. My girlfriend Robin was one, a bohemian aristocrat in my eyes. Six feet tall and silent in a mysterious, pliant way, she inspired the attention of older men, who were a constant threat to me. She grew up on Bleecker Street and hung out at the Village coffee houses and at the Kettle of Fish Tavern on MacDougal Street, where the folk singer Dave Van Ronk drank between sets at the Gaslight downstairs.

I fell for Robin's family almost as hard as I did for her. They were physically imposing, idealistic, and rebellious but with an overlay of gentility—the antidote to what I thought of as my vulgar, provincial-minded clan.

Her father, Robert DeCormier, was a musician with a deep knowledge of the traditional American folk canon: rebel ballads, spirituals, work songs, hymns. He had studied voice and conducting at Juilliard on the GI bill after being wounded in France during the Second World War. His attraction to folk music was political. It was the word from below, populist not pop, the voice of the working man.

He became Harry Belafonte's musical director after Belafonte's hit Caribbean album in 1956. Bob would transcribe songs from Alan Lomax's Library of Congress recordings, field songs such as "Swing Dat Hammer." "I'd arrange them for the singers. Twelve voices. The Belafonte Singers, we were called. It boggled the mind that grass-roots ethnological music could sell in the millions." By the time I met Bob, he was touring with his own group, in a rented bus six months a year. He transformed old-time roustabout songs into choral compositions that came at you with a liturgical dignity, dense and precise.

Robin's family welcomed me into the fold, though I suspect Bob considered me flimsy material for his daughter. I certainly felt insubstantial compared to the virtuoso musicians who came round to their apartment. Some of these musicians had an aura about them, like athletes, as if an essential aspect of their being was in abeyance between gigs. I wanted to approach writing the same way: chops up, and ready to pour forth when it counted.

I listened to folk music in those days the way I read Willa Cather or Mark Twain: with the idea that I was getting information about the "authentic" America that I wanted to belong to but as a New York Jew didn't really believe that I did. Folk music was underground news from the heartland, or so I believed. "I been blastin', I been firin',/I been pourin' red-hot iron." It was elemental and brawny in a way that the saloon singers whom my parents listened to were not. When Tony Bennett crooned "Baby, Ain't I Good to You" I could hear the tuxedo in his voice, though I understood that it might be rented and would have to be returned in the morning.

After a while, I realized that my notion of the dichotomy between New York and "authentic" America was outdated. By the late 1960s, folk music had passed into the hands of preservationists, city players for the most part, who were picking it up second hand. Ramblin' Jack Elliott, Woody Guthrie's protégé, was really Elliot Charles Adnopoz, the son of a prominent New York surgeon. "I was born on a 45,000-acre ranch in the middle of Brooklyn," he once confessed, knowing that people believed he was a cowhand. Moe Asch, the founder of Folkways records, was the son of the Yiddish novelist Sholem Asch. Dave Van Ronk was from Brooklyn. "He was the one performer I burned to learn particulars from," Bob Dylan writes in his memoir, *Chronicles*. "He turned every folk song into a surreal melodrama, a theatrical piece . . . it was like he had an endless supply of poison and I wanted some. . . . I couldn't do without it."

Van Ronk's prize student was Danny Kalb, whose guitar style was watery and fast, folk-blues with an unpredictability that was related to jazz. In 1967, I lined up outside the Cafe Au Go Go to hear Danny play with his band, the Blues Project. A couple of years later I found out that he had been Robin's boyfriend before Robin and I met. She had probably been backstage that night. By the time Danny and I became friends, his career was in decline. One night he played a blues ballad for Robin and me in our apartment. "Mean Old Southern

Railroad," it was called. "Caught her standin' in the rain with her feet soakin' wet/Beggin' each and every man she met." When Danny was eighteen, he had sung the song for a live radio broadcast from Riverside Church on the Upper West Side. Dylan, who was enthralled by Danny's guitar-playing, accompanied him on harmonica.

I phone Danny now to see how he's getting along, the first time we have spoken in years. "Everything has changed, Michael," he says. "I'm a different person now. I've shifted from the Far Left to the Far Right. It's a new world."

He tells me he is writing a memoir entitled, *My Life, the Sixties, Muddy Waters, and God.* I picture him in his tiny Brooklyn apartment, pecking away at the computer, trying to make sense of the crack-up that caused him to retreat from the music scene.

"Do I owe you any money?" he asks.

I dimly remember an outstanding debt for a couple of hundred bucks.

"Sorry if I treated you bad," he says, and abruptly hangs up.

As if to complete the conversation, I immediately phone Robin. She owns a bakery with her new husband in Vermont and is exhausted after a day's work. "Who can remember these things, Michael," she says good-naturedly. "And who cares?"

Later, I reach her father, Bob, who is happy to indulge me. His voice throws me back to adolescence when I saw him as a kind of god. He was one of the first adults to encourage me as a writer. Eighty-three now, he is directing a new group of singers. "We just recorded an album of Yiddish songs called *When the Rabbi Danced.*"

MY ELDER SON Aaron is twenty-nine today, and over a commemorative drink I tease him about his reluctance to be born: two weeks late, after twenty-six hours of labor, until he finally popped out weighing more than ten pounds and looking like a cross between Sonny Liston and Nikita Khrushchev. "A case of rational resistance," remarks Aaron, who has heard this story before.

I was twenty-one when he was born, and the events that led to my becoming a father at that age seem like something from a half-remembered dream. As an aspiring writer, I figured I would do well to experience a place other than New York and so, with money salted away from a job at a Manhattan post office, I lit out for South America with my high school girlfriend Robin. She had been about to start college and was reluctant to come along. Inward-looking by temperament, Robin had little desire for the kind of blunt exotic experience

I sought. Anxious not to go it alone, however, I persuaded her to join me.

It was the early 1970s, the prime of the Latin American literary boom. An aura of promise and political chaos pervaded the continent, and part of its attraction was that the two seemed to go hand in hand. My idea was that North and South were inextricably entwined, the extension and flip side of each other, the alpha and omega of the New World. Borges, with his metaphysical tales, was connected to Hawthorne and Poe. García Márquez was heir to Faulkner.

With the hope of tapping into this current, I decided we should settle in Buenos Aires. I was told that the way to meet Borges there was to use the pretext of his blindness to accompany him across the street when he emerged from the National Library where he worked. It proved to be good advice. Within seconds of my introducing myself, he guessed that I was from New York, and then, with the confident divination of his blindness, that I was Jewish, a tribalism whose bloodline, he assured me, he shared by a demonstrable quarter.

Borges was seventy-four, but his soft pale face, his slightly Castilian lisp, and his unshielded, upward-floating eyes gave him a childlike air. Lamenting Argentina's deteriorating political situation, he employed the same words he had once used to describe going blind: "It is like watching a slow sunset."

Argentina was much in the world news and it wasn't difficult for me to find work as a stringer writing for various publications back home. Within a year of our arrival, the country was at the point of civil war. I was electrified by the turmoil, though I should have been alarmed. Robin, for her part, was uninterested in politics, studying Argentine music and acting in an experimental play in which she had been cast for her elongated, strikingly Klimt-like figure. Late at night we would lie awake in our apartment, listening to gunshots and the explosion of homemade bombs.

One evening Robin visited a friend who was convalescing from a minor illness in the hospital. Leaving the hospital, she stumbled on a demonstration in the Congressional Plaza. As she ran from the tear gas, she was apprehended.

The next morning her picture was in the papers, one of several members of a "revolutionary cell." "Confiscated arms" were displayed. The ringleader, so the official story went, had been killed by police while trying to blast his way out of the precinct jail, sparking a revolt. There was a photograph of his body on the gray patio stone. Robin and her fellow "guerrilleros" were to be transported to an undisclosed location.

I tramped from one police station to another for three days until I found her, in a tiny cell on the outskirts of the city. When I appealed to the United States consul for help, he told me that with seven thousand dollars in cash I would be able to gain her immediate release. "This is the police chief's price, not mine," he added. I managed to scrape up about nine hundred bucks, enough to buy the assistance of the captain of the local firehouse, who was able to have Robin formally charged with disorderly conduct.

The so-called prison revolt, I learned, had been staged by police to cover up the murder, during interrogation, of a young man whose well-to-do parents had powerful political connections. When the police opened fire, dozens of bullets sprayed through the bars of Robin's cell, missing her because a fellow prisoner had pushed her to the ground.

On the morning of Robin's release, I met her in front of the jail. Waiting families congratulated us, then watched forlornly as we walked together down the concrete ramp. That evening, we took a steamship across the River Plate to Montevideo. We traveled through the Uruguayan countryside in silence, clutching each other as we stared out at the plains.

For a week we holed up in a town called Fray Bentos, hardly leaving the tiny inn where we stayed. We were twenty years old. Our future as a couple was fragile. We had never discussed having a child, but we made love in a kind of lustless trance, as if asserting ourselves against death and the random terror of the world.

It was only later that I connected Fray Bentos to Borges's story "Funes the Memorious," which takes place in that town. Funes is a teenage boy, the son of an ironing woman and an unknown father. Thrown by a wild horse, he is "hopelessly crippled." Upon regaining consciousness, he is startled by the bright richness of the world, which he finds to be "almost intolerable." His perception is so precise that every instant generates the memory of itself, as vivid as the original experience it recalls. There is no area of obscurity in his mind. "He remembered the shapes of the clouds in the south at dawn on the 30th of April, and he could compare them in his recollection with the marbled grain in the design of a leather-bound book which he had seen only once. . . .

"He could continuously make out the tranquil advances of corruption, of caries, of fatigue. . . . Two or three times he had reconstructed an entire day."

Robin and I were the opposite: abstracted, somnolent, conceiving our son in a daze, with little thought of the future or the past. We returned to New York before Aaron was born, and split up some years later. On the rare occasions when we speak of our week in Fray Bentos, all we can remember are the shutters on the inn's window, the patio with its broken tiles, and a thick overhead vine that kept us in a state of soothing semidarkness.

Milk and Honey

AN UNEXPECTED PHONE CALL throws me back to the tiny Hebrew day school I attended between the ages of five and thirteen. "Are you the Michael Greenberg who went to Beth-El?" asks the voice on the other end of the line. When I say that I am, the caller identifies himself as my former class-mate, Ira. I immediately remember him for his bright red hair and studious ways. "I managed to track down five others," he says. "We're planning to get together next week." He gives me the name of a restaurant near Union Square.

The days leading up to our rendezvous are filled with flashes of that insular world. The school was in Rockaway, a thin spit of urban coastland separated from Brooklyn by a drawbridge. None of us came from especially religious homes, yet there we were for eight years, crawling through every word of the Five Books of Moses, in Hebrew. Four hours a day were devoted to this task, while three hours were given over to the examination of "social studies" and English. As for mathematics, one picked up almost enough to get by as a shopkeeper or small-time entrepreneur, which many of our parents were. Science wasn't offered because no one on the faculty knew how to teach it.

Several of our teachers were refugees from Europe, and I sometimes wondered if they would have been able to make a living outside the school. Tempers were short; it wasn't unusual for some of the teachers to lose control completely. One was given to explosive attacks on us for minor infractions such as talking out of turn. To keep himself in check, he wore a brass whistle around his neck, which he would blow furiously, his eyes bulging. Another regularly pulled us around the classroom by our ears. We were more bewildered than frightened by these outbursts; they seemed to come out of an inner turmoil that we had no hope of comprehending.

But under the right circumstances, we too knew how to be cruel. Though it was never mentioned in school, we were aware that our second-grade Torah instructor had been a prisoner at Auschwitz; his inmate number was visible on his arm. Alert to any sign of adult weakness, we imitated his stammer, exploiting his aura of exhaustion and premature old age. We were American-born, exempt from the genocide and ignorant of his ordeal. Our families had fled Europe before the First World War. My grandfather, for example, had so thoroughly cut his ties with the Old Country that he never even told my father his real name; his "shtetl name," he called it. I still don't know what it was. It took the televised Eichmann trial in 1961 for me to get an idea of what had really happened in Europe.

Guilt about their relatively easy lives, I believe, was why our parents sent us to Beth-El. There was a discreet pressure after the war for us to do our bit for the prolongation of the tribe. In a way, the impracticality of our schooling was proof of its value, though my father would have been appalled if I had taken the Torah too much to heart. After leaving, I was expected to join the American hustle like everyone else. When I demonstrated a modest talent for the study of talmudic law, my teachers encouraged me to consider a career as a rabbi. Indignant, my father ordered them to back off.

The day of our gathering at the restaurant arrives. Seven of us show up, half of our graduating class. After the predictable shock of seeing our fixed childhood image of one another shattered by middle age, we order drinks and get down to the business of remembering and filling in the years. A warm feeling arises; we want to think well of each other. None of us, I note, is religious. We are all partial Jews.

Phyllis, animated, emphatic, is in New York to promote her recently published cookbook, which includes, she says, "dishes inspired by biblical times," such as chicken with figs. "I moved to Tel Aviv and married Simon Peres's son just when his father was running for prime minister. The marriage lasted nine months." She leans forward as she speaks, at one point pressing my hand to scold me for never trying to make out with her. "You had your chances," she says.

Martha, glamorous, gym-toned, remembers without rancor schoolyard games where "every day I had to endure the same ritual of rejection." She is a divorce lawyer now, specializing in high-profile cases. "We represented Donald Trump's wife," she says, leaving us to imagine the melodrama and millions involved.

Mindy runs a school for handicapped children in the Catskills. "I've turned into a hick," she says. Her memory is more detailed than that of the rest of us: she evokes the hurricane of 1960, when Rockaway flooded and we drifted ecstatically through the streets on ruined furniture which we had turned into rafts. She recalls the ominous gang of boys I organized whose mission was to wrap the thorn bushes that grew through the schoolyard fence around the girls. We tore our fingers trapping them, while they were scratched like martyrs when they tried to break free. I was relieved when the principal threatened expulsion if we continued our game. That was the same year we tormented our teacher from Auschwitz.

David, a building contractor now, still lives in the old neighborhood, a few blocks from the school. I am not surprised when he tells me that it closed down in the 1970s. It only lasted about twenty years. It hadn't been pious enough to appeal to the truly Orthodox, yet it wasn't particularly forward-looking either. When our teachers died, there seemed to be no one to replace them. It was an ambivalent creature of that brief postwar time.

The restaurant dims its lights and we wander out onto Union Square. A subtle feeling of protectiveness toward one another has settled over us, the protectiveness, perhaps, of the adult toward the child. Phyllis heads off in search of copies of her cookbook to sign. "With my signature in them, they can't be returned," she explains. Jeffrey, in perfect pitch, sings snippets of a familiar Hebrew prayer. He is an architect now, but all I see is the dizzy sparkle he had as a boy, when an air of chaos seemed perpetually to surround him. "The meaning is lost on me," he says of the prayer. "All I remember is the music. The rhythm of those esoteric words."

A Tailor's Fortune

I HAVE BEEN VISITING MY MOTHER this week at an East Side hospital where she is recovering from surgery. Each time I go up to her room on the eighth floor I think of Jakov Schoenloz, my former Lower East Side neighbor who was brought to the same hospital in 1985 after suffering a heart attack in the East Broadway subway station near the building where we lived. Jakov—or Jack as he called himself in New York—was born in Lodz, in 1922, the same year as my mother, though their fortunes in every other respect could not have been more different. Jack was a minute, unnoticeable figure, with a forkful of gray-brown hair, a parched voice, and thick tortoiseshell glasses that he seemed constantly to be repairing with a tube of glue and a paper clip. His father had taught him to be a tailor, a trade that Jack said had saved his life on more than one occasion.

In 1940 he was cleaning toilets in the administrative offices of the Burgermeister when a Nazi official advised him to clear out of Poland without delay. Jack made it to the Soviet-controlled border at Bialystok, where a Russian guard let him through in exchange for his sweater. His skill with the sewing needle landed him a relatively benign position in a sweatshop in Uzbekistan, where he lived through the war with no idea of what was taking place in Europe.

Returning to Lodz in 1946, Jack discovered that he was the only member of his family who was still alive. He moved around Europe for a while, throwing himself into what he called "the gutter life of a petty black marketeer," and then, in the early 1960s, settled in New York.

When we met in 1978, he was working in the basement of Macy's department store, hemming trousers and letting out waistlines. We stood out as the palest tenants in our enormous, government-subsidized apartment complex on Cherry Street. One night I invited him for dinner, and he showed up with a store-bought cherry pie. Thereafter he dropped by whenever he pleased, which wasn't often. He wore a baggy woolen sweater twelve months of the year, and his ill-fitting shirts were alteration jobs from Macy's that had never been claimed. He had a rare capacity for solitude, and a feeling of misanthropy that seemed to run so deep I wondered if it was innate rather than a scar from his wartime misfortune. He confided in me that only once had he slept with a woman he didn't pay for—a terrifying experience because their lovemaking seemed to imply a promise that he had no ability to fulfill. It was a mark of his honesty and good will, he believed, that he didn't pretend tenderness where there was none.

When I came to see him in the hospital after his heart attack, he told me in an urgent, whispery voice: "I've put away a lot of money. You should have it. I don't want it to go to waste." He asked me to write out the bequest for him to sign right there, though in his agitation he could barely make himself heard. I thought he was imagining the money and, as always with the mortally sick, I regretted shoving my good health in front of his nose. "We'll take care of it tomorrow," I said. "The nurses want you to rest." The next day I learned that Jack had died during the night.

I realized that I had underestimated the meaning of his visits to us. Remembering his extreme frugality—motivated less by meanness, it seemed, than by an ethos of self-deprivation that was second nature to him—I felt sure that the money he had spoken of existed. It was moving to think that, knowing I was broke, Jack had wanted me to have it. But why had he waited until almost the moment of his death to make the announcement?

I did nothing for two or three weeks, then one day I spotted a letter addressed to Jack lying by the mailbox. It was from Bank Hapoalim in Israel. The building superintendent had scrawled the word "deceased" on the envelope and left it for the mail carrier to retrieve. I swiped the letter and opened it in my apartment.

It was a routine notification that Jack's ninety-day certificate of deposit in the amount of $107,344 was due to mature. The bank would renew it, unless Jack instructed them to do otherwise. I berated myself for having denied Jack the satisfaction of knowing his dying wish would be fulfilled, and imagined "my" money lost in an eternal interest-accruing orbit.

A couple of months later, a man named Miller came to see me. He had heard from "people in the building" that I was "a close associate of Jack." Would I mind answering a few questions? Accompanying Miller was a man in his early fifties called Chaim, with a slight tremor that suggested an early stage of Parkinson's disease. Miller explained that Chaim was the son of Jack's sister and the only other family member to have come out of the Holocaust alive. "I'm representing him. He doesn't talk English," said Miller.

Chaim had traveled from Israel to be present at the reading of Jack's will, of which Chaim was the sole beneficiary. I dimly remembered Jack speaking with resentment of him, after he had tracked Jack down and contacted him for the first and last time. Jack had turned him away. He said that he had come to grips with the complete obliteration of his bloodline; he had lived as if "there was no one." To learn suddenly that his nephew had been alive all the while, threatened to tear apart "what little I built of myself" since the war.

Referring to Chaim, Miller said, "You should know that this man is a child alumnus of Auschwitz." And at this, he launched into a diatribe against Jack. "Do you have any idea of the cruelty of that bastard who you called your friend?" Jack's will had directed Chaim to a safety deposit box at a bank on Grand Street. The box was empty, except for a set of false teeth, painted gold.

"For what reason, this ugliness?" asked Miller. "What did he stand to gain?"

I handed Chaim the letter from Bank Hapoalim, with the odd sense that Jack had arranged things so I would play exactly this role. A hasty deathbed bequest would have been of dubious legal value. Chaim was the heir of record. "You should have no trouble claiming this," I said.

Miller seemed caught between astonishment, delight, and new heights of indignation. He threatened to have the postal inspector investigate me for tampering with the mail. Then he shook my hand vigorously and hurried away with Chaim.

GROWING UP, MY SON AARON seemed able to make sense of social enigmas that I, with my comparatively sheltered upbringing, had not even known existed. In my tightly knit neighborhood non-Jews had been exotic to me, the mysterious Other. My first black friend ran off with my overcoat while we were reading comic books at the local soda shop, and assiduously shunned me thereafter. The Irish gangs across the avenue were a constant source of fear. Aaron, by contrast, seems able to talk to anyone with ease. He is fluent in the language of the street and in the language of the parlor, sliding effortlessly between them as the situation demands.

In 1978, when Aaron was three, we moved into a twenty-six-story public housing project on Cherry Street at the border of Chinatown and the Lower East Side. The tenants of the building had been chosen to reflect the ethnic composition of the surrounding streets: 35 percent Hispanic, 30 percent

Chinese, 30 percent black. Apart from us, there were three other white people in the project, all of them elderly Jews living alone, holdovers from the neighborhood's previous incarnation.

Living there was yet another way to subsidize my writing, while I worked at a series of dead-end jobs that stood no chance of threatening my fragile literary identity. By settling in the projects, however, I abdicated my status as a tenement-dwelling artist. We became unglamorously poor, an embarrassing state, since, unlike my new neighbors, I had a father who was a solid member of the middle class.

As the only white boy in the building, Aaron was vulnerable to racial derision. In the playground he was called "Chucky," after a white, cherubic, horror-movie demon. I watched him develop a wary strut and a radar for detecting violence that I both worried about and admired. I often kept an eye on him while he played basketball with an older crowd on the cement court behind our building. While a player was wrestling for a rebound one day, a silver handgun fell out of his jeans, a gleaming semi-automatic. Aaron seemed unfazed. Shortly afterward, we moved away, into a fifth-story walk-up apartment on a tranquil block across town.

On a scholarship, Aaron attended a tiny socialist high school in Greenwich Village that boasted among its alumni Angela Davis, Kathy Boudin, and the orphans of the executed communists Julius and Ethel Rosenberg. I had gone to the school briefly as well, in the eleventh grade, and had met Aaron's mother Robin there. With the decline of the Left, it had become just another exclusive Manhattan enclave. Of Aaron's closest friends, one was heir to the Barbie Doll fortune; another described his father to me as "a close associate of Jack Nicholson."

After college, Aaron joined the Peace Corps and went to Eritrea. On his return to New York, he ran a training program for foster children with the Administration for Child Services in the Bronx, a government-sponsored version of hell: "Punched out walls, kids lying around, paid caregivers dealing crack, everyone hammered into the ground." His feeling for the have-nots seemed instinctual and pragmatic, driven by a complicated intimacy.

A couple of years later he was back in Africa, in Sierra Leone this time, working in refugee camps near the Liberian border. We conversed by satellite phone, the sound of rain on a metal roof in the background like skittering paws, while Aaron told me about refugee riots, diamond mines, and the fall of Charles Taylor.

Enthralled by his adventures, while stuck at my desk in New York, I urged him to keep a journal. Aaron didn't see the point in it. He wasn't interested in wringing stories from his life. For him, experience was to be had, not told.

Last month, he received a graduate degree in International Affairs, and now he is searching for a job with the UN or an international NGO, hoping to land again in Africa or Asia. I visit him at his office in the turreted arsenal on Fifth Avenue at 64th Street in Central Park, where he is temporarily organizing recreational events for the city. His window overlooks the seal pond in the zoo, its fringes crusted with snow, the seals animated and barking in the cold. Aaron is tense about his job hunt, and fed up with his current position, which he finds unchallenging. However, his prospects are limited by the fact that he is American with a name that pegs him as Jewish. This makes him an enticing kidnap target, a factor that organizations consider when sending people into the field.

I feel moved to apologize for this ethnic curse, since to Jews Aaron isn't one—his mother is a shiksa—and I did not provide him with even the rudiments of religion, much less a sense of Zionist morale. "I've given you all the drawbacks with none of the perks," I say. Aaron surprises me, however, by declaring that he thinks of himself as a Jew. "A New York Jew, a vague identity. Rootless and freeing." Delighted, I repeat the critic Harold Rosenberg's definition of the New York Jew: one caught in a particular net of "memory and expectation."

At lunch, Aaron remembers an incident from his days in Eritrea. He was teaching classes of seventy-five students or more. He had vowed not to beat his students or make them kneel in the sun while holding rocks over their heads, as was common practice at the school. "I told the other teachers I would show them a better way to keep order, but they laughed at me, and the truth is my class was out of control. One day, Den-Den, a seventeen-year-old and the worst of the lot, threw a stone at my best student, knocking her out cold. I lost my head completely, beating the hell out of the kid, then dragging him into the principal's office, his face bloody and his clothes torn."

Aaron was disgusted with himself. But the following day he was greeted by his fellow teachers as a hero. They presented him with a stick, the "tool" he had rejected when he first arrived at the school. The boy's mother publicly thanked him for beating her son. His students became respectful and quiet.

Listening to him, I feel like the narrator of Hemingway's story "In Another Country." My son is a hunting hawk. I am not one. "Although I might seem a hawk to those who have never hunted."

Sleight of Hand

MY PARENTAL FEELINGS are unexpectedly aroused by Henry, the young man who works at the small coffee bar where I get my daily fix of caffeine. Henry reminds me of my elder son Aaron. They are almost the same age, wear their woolen caps at a similarly satirical angle, and share, I think, a pleasantly gregarious approach to the world.

Henry's parents split when he was a boy, and, like my son under similar circumstances, Henry moved in with his father. "We lived in a one-bedroom apartment, with a sofa bed in the living room," he says, giving an accurate description of my own post-divorce pad. His father is a magician, a profession that I imagine to be more precarious even than that of writer. "When I was four, he used to pull me out of his hat instead of a rabbit," says Henry. His father's crowd-pleaser was to toss an entire deck of cards in the air, thrusting his knife through a pre-chosen card before it hit the floor. "I'd tell you how he does it," Henry says, "but that would violate the magician's code."

Henry confides his troubles to me, most of which involve a chronic lack of cash. He wants to marry the French au pair who often comes into the shop, but the filing fee for citizenship is $1,850, and they are trying to scrape up enough money to rent an apartment.

One morning, he hands me my coffee and rings up $1.25 on the cash register instead of the usual cost, two dollars. With a brazen, slightly grudging look he gives me seventy-five cents in change, which I automatically drop into his tip jar. In this momentary exchange, a vague sense of complicity is established between us. Or is it? Later, I wonder if I am reading too much into what happened. It was probably just a mistake, Henry distractedly ringing up the price of a small coffee instead of a large one.

The next morning, however, he undercharges me for my coffee again. This time I resist transferring the change to his tip jar, as I am certain he expects me to do. Closing my fist around the coins, I debate whether to confront him. Several people are standing in line behind me, waiting to be served. To bring up the subject in front of them, I decide, would be worse punishment than the infringement deserves. I leave the coffee bar with the change, realizing that I am the one who has benefited from this transaction, at the expense of his boss.

So he's skimming a few pennies. I think, what difference does it make? The urge to steal must be irresistible, given his low wages and the fact that the owner of the coffee bar spends most of the day at his other store. I remember working at a small bookshop when I was in my late teens. Casting myself as the exploited worker, I once pocketed the proceeds from a sale. The owner of the bookshop reminded me of my father, sweating the details of his business, dismissive of everything that didn't relate to the narrow world of his affairs. *Steal This Book* by Abbie Hoffman was a best seller that year; Henry has the corporate swindlers of Enron and AIG to look up to. We both ripped off our bosses with no thought of what it cost them to stay in business. Today, bookshops like the one I worked at don't exist in Manhattan and I think of my petty larceny as a lasting personal stain.

I avoid the coffee bar for a couple of days, and when I show up again, Henry is glowing. "I got married," he announces. He shows me pictures of the wedding: City Hall on a slushy winter morning, Henry in a black T-shirt with a red tie knotted comically around his neck, his bride in jeans and a white pullover, clutching a bunch of half-frozen carnations. This time he rings up my coffee without short-changing the owner. Relieved, I stuff twenty bucks in his tip jar: a wedding gift.

When I return later that afternoon, however, the drawer of the cash register is open and Henry takes my money without bothering to record the sale. Clearly he is doing this with other customers as well, bleeding the store, which will have to shut down if he continues, leaving me with no place to go but Starbucks, where unauthorized contact with money by an employee is apt to set off security alarms.

The CD player is blasting, and Henry's wife, the French au pair, and several of their friends are singing along. "My father's performing tonight, if you want to catch his act," shouts Henry over the music. He writes down the address of a place somewhere out in Long Island.

I arrive late at the rundown club and nod curtly to Henry who is sitting alone on the other side of the room. The first performer does elaborate rope tricks, then reads the mind of an audience member who I suspect is his girlfriend.

Next, an elderly man with a blond hairpiece performs a complicated card trick involving queens, which he refers to as "our ladies of the night," and jacks, which he calls "their johns." By the time he spreads his arms to indicate the trick is over, the audience is completely baffled. Henry slouches in his seat and covers his face with his hands.

Finally, his father takes the stage, a mild, ingratiating man in his fifties. His delivery is more polished than that of the others as he performs an impressive sleight of hand with three cups and different-colored balls. For his coup de grace he takes a wad of bills from an audience member and—poof!—makes the money disappear.

When Henry slips out of the club for a smoke, I follow, standing next to him in the cold. "I've been watching this stuff all my life," he says, a little sadly.

With a stab of recognition, I think of Aaron scrutinizing my ups and downs as a writer. I have worked out what to say to Henry, not wanting to sound accusatory or self-righteous. But what comes out of my mouth is: "Get your hands out of the till or I am going to tell your boss."

He looks at me with surprise, then with a glimmer of hatred. "It wasn't costing you anything. I thought you were on my side."

I thought so too. But I was just playing a trick on myself.

CLARENCE PHONES to give me the good news: he has landed a job as motorman on the New York City subway, the consummation of a lifelong romance with trains. The rare note of excitement in his voice delights me. I have known Clarence since he was ten years old, a timid boy who would spend hours with my son Aaron hunkered over the Lego blocks they both loved to play with. Since then, we have kept in touch intermittently— at his request, I would cook up the occasional job recommendation and he would fill me in on how he was getting along. In recent years, I've watched him grow into a solemn, increasingly reclusive young man. He lives alone in the same Harlem apartment where he grew up, an only child. His powerful body, augmented by weightlifting and a complicated array of high-protein drinks, gives him a vaguely explosive air. His latest job, at a local drugstore chain, ended when he accused the chairman of running the company "like a slave ship."

To Clarence the subway has always been less a means of conveyance than a destination in itself. As a teenager he would gaze out the window of the front car, studying the various signals and switches, teaching himself to "read the iron." In Riverside Park one day, he discovered an entrance to the underground tracks for the long-distance passenger trains that come in and out of Penn Station. He would walk the tracks to the northern tip of Manhattan while the locomotives blew by, making him feel, he once said, like he was being "lifted off the ground." Sunlight through the vents would reveal the so-called "mole people" who lived down there, a rank collection of outcasts who sharpened Clarence's sense of the city's tunnels as an esoteric world, known only to the initiated few.

"I've been operating for five months," he tells me now on the phone, "but I didn't want to call you till I was certain the job was mine." I accept his invitation to ride with him the following day, Christmas. "I'll be working the lobster shift," he informs me. "Four p.m. to midnight."

I meet up with Clarence at Pelham Bay in the Bronx, an outdoor station with a cutting wind on its elevated platform. He greets me in his blue motorman's uniform and a crimson Santa hat topped with a furry snow-white ball. "Merry Christmas!" he shouts. I have never seen him so confident or at ease. He will be operating one of the newest trains in the system, he says, "the R142, a soda can on wheels." He shows me into the motorman's cab with its cushioned seat and computerized trouble screen that tells you "everything except if a passenger's sleeve is caught in the door." Clarence inserts two long-bladed skeleton keys into the control panel, releases the brake, and the soda can slides forward, a little tentative on the icy rails.

The view from the cab is thrilling: diamond switches on the tracks being swallowed beneath us, steel dust pouring from the rails, a cross made of gnarled bones in a passing apartment window. Clarence is intent, and mostly silent, careful not to lose face by overshooting the stations.

As we cross the Harlem River and lay into the long downgrade to Manhattan, he brings the train up to fifty-three miles per hour and breaks into a huge smile. In the tunnel, it's a different world. On the coarse, bedrock walls shines the byzantine tag of Zane Smith, a graffiti artist whose penetration into the subway's most inaccessible shafts remains a source of wonder. To Clarence, the graffiti is a comforting sight, cave drawings from the prehistoric 1970s, when ungoverned trains got up to 70 mph, flaggers openly smoked ganja on the job, and maintenance crews ripped spikes from one section of track to repair another.

Relatively few trains are running today and the signals are green all the way to Brooklyn Bridge, where we turn round and head back uptown. I leave Clarence's cab to wander through the cars. At Astor Place, a woman with delirious red hair and two large suitcases clatters aboard. She removes her platform shoes, props her feet on the suitcases, and falls asleep, snoring. At 96th Street she bolts awake and hurriedly disembarks. This is the unofficial color line; north of here is East Harlem. At 125th Street the middle cars fill up for the Bronx leg of our journey. An off-duty security guard performs a brief James Brown impersonation, then plops, out of breath, into the arms of his companion.

When the train emerges again onto the elevated tracks, we stir like people in a room where the blinds have suddenly been opened. Cell phones pipe up, each with its customized ring. The young man sitting next to me writes intensely in his notebook. I look over his shoulder and read: "I'm in love with my best friend's wife/she calls me when they get into fights/he calls me when he needs a crib for the night."

At Parkchester Avenue the car empties and I am alone except for two mariachi guitarists splitting their tips on the seat between them. Clarence eases us into Pelham Bay, the end of the line. The brakes dump their air with a colossal sigh.

Eight p.m., lunchtime. With difficulty we find a deli that is open and return to the station. To get out of the cold, Clarence unlocks a storage room filled with scrub brooms and several gallons of disinfectant. While we eat, he tells me about the blackout last August, right in the middle of evening rush hour, his first week operating without an instructor. The conductor led the passengers out the nearest escape hatch, while Clarence was ordered to stay with his train. It was pitch black, infernally hot, and silent except for the occasional tinkle of water dripping from the beams. He was asleep when the power came on with a hum like a swarm of bees. "The blast from the air conditioner made my teeth chatter, I was so soaked with sweat. Then I heard the first train move somewhere down the line. It sounded like thunder."

At home that night I listen to Duke Ellington's "Take the 'A' Train" with its hard swing and echoing bell-chord like a subway horn.

The next morning I phone Clarence to thank him for the ride. "I never thought this could happen to me," he says. "Doing what I love on Christmas. And earning double time."

"Oh! Oh! There He Goes!"

THE RAT PROBLEM on our street on the Upper West Side is finally under control. Last spring, however, it overwhelmed us. Late at night, the red cedars in their tree boxes in front of our building were bristling with rats. A dog was bit on the nose after trapping one along the lumber store's front wall. In June, I spotted a couple in broad daylight, dashing up the side of an uncovered trash can, ripping open a black plastic bag, and plunging inside it. This was a bad sign; it meant that they had multiplied to the point where the food supply was stretched and weaker rats were obliged to take their chances by day.

A few weeks later, I stood at my window after midnight, watching them scoop water from the curb with their front paws. Dozens of them were hanging out like teenagers, copulating, browsing, completely at ease. Released from their usual panicked state, a new arrogance was revealed. When crossing paths with them, I felt a shiver of recognition, and hatred. I thought of Seamus Heaney's poem "An Advancement of Learning." A rat "slobbered curtly, close,/Smudging the silence . . ." The poet "sickened so quickly that/I turned down the path in cold sweat." Heaney's rat ran up a sewer pipe. Mine stayed put, staring me down and snarling.

The common brown Norway rat is the urban equivalent of Grimm's wolf, skittering down the street with its long yellow teeth, nimbling through tiny holes in the pavement, and rising up again through a gnawed piece of flooring. Rats exist in a magnified state of unease that seems to be a grotesque version of our own.

One of the most unforgivable things about them is how much they remind us of ourselves. Their sexual appetite appears to be driven more by anxiety than procreative need (a male rat will mate twenty times in a day). They will eat themselves into a stupor, and exercise until they drop dead from exhaustion. Rats are highly sensitive to one another's moods: a single stressed adult will transmit anxiety through a relatively peaceful nest like an electric wire. Their favorite food is peanut butter, but in a pinch they can live off almost anything, including machine grease, oil paint, rubber, paste, and, as a last resort, each other. They appear to take pleasure in acts of vandalism, and will lay waste to an entire grocery store for a couple of ounces of food. Occasionally they fall into ecstatic killing sprees. Joseph Mitchell writes of a burrow of rats in the poultry market at the old Gansevoort Market in the early 1940s: "They bit the throats of over three hundred broilers and ate less than a dozen."

Returning home late at night last spring, my neighbors and I would walk in the middle of the street, anxiously striking the ground with umbrellas or sticks, stamping our feet, hoping to make the rats scatter. They ignored us. The tables were turned; they weren't on the run for a change, and they seemed to want to mock us. We had the sense that we were tainted in some way. We had lost face, had failed to hold our own. The barbarians had overrun us.

In August, the exterminators came, baited the burrows with poison, and the surviving rats went back underground. However, I have been unable to get them out of my mind. Are there really fewer rats on the subway tracks than before? "Track rabbits," the transit workers call them. Along with most New Yorkers, I used to believe that there were at least eight million rats in the city, one for every human being. I am comforted now to read of a study that puts their population at no more than 250,000. Despite my memory of some the size of small dogs, the Norway rat rarely weighs more than a pound. And while their natural life span is three to four years, in New York few make it half that long.

Nevertheless, I keep thinking I see them, rushing past, out the corner of my eye. They seem to pop up everywhere, and not just live ones. On Broadway, over the main gate of Columbia University, looms a giant inflatable rat, a protest against nonunion hiring at the school. It takes four men with ropes to hold the rat down, fat, droopy-eyed, cartoonishly vicious.

The grip of rats on my consciousness is strong enough for me to feel mildly phobic about them, and greatly disturbed when they appear in my dreams. Freud's remark that rats in dreams often stand for the dreamer's siblings has haunted me for years. I grew up in a nest of five brothers, a hard-headed father, and a mother whose attentions were fought over with paranoiac ferocity. When I was a young boy, one older brother seemed especially rat-like: nervously abrupt in his movements, greedy, accusing, insidiously smart. When trained on me, his eyes had an opaque, humorless gloss.

One of Freud's most famous patients temporarily confounded the doctor with his "strange and senseless obsessions about rats." The case of the Rat Man. During analysis it emerged that to him rats signified, among other things, money, violence, anal eroticism, babies, infectious disease, and corporal punishment. When visiting his father's grave, he sees a rat scurry past and assumes that it has been feeding on his father's corpse. Rat Man had been a biter himself as a child, for which he was severely beaten by his father. In the case history, Freud writes: "He has often watched, horror struck, as a rat was cruelly hunted down and ruthlessly killed by human beings." Upon seeing in the rat "a living likeness of himself," Freud claims, the patient's "rat delirium" went away.

I remember, in the late 1960s, when hundreds of rats appeared on Park Avenue just north of Midtown. They were destroying the tulips, running brazenly down the traffic island in the middle of the avenue. The *New York Times* suggested that they might be "refugees from Harlem." Maybe they had in mind the opening scene of Richard Wright's novel *Native Son*. On seeing a rat in his apartment, Bigger Thomas is "galvanized into violent action." The rat "leaped at Bigger's trouser leg, snagging it in his teeth, hanging on." Bigger swings an iron skillet at the creature. His sister runs into a corner, holding the hem of her slip "tightly over her knees. 'Oh! Oh!' she wailed. 'There he goes!'"

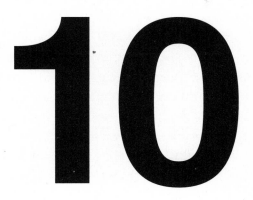

HAVING A COUPLE OF HOURS to kill on the Lower East Side, I wander into the Tenement Museum at 97 Orchard Street. Five choked railroad flats have been re-created with a realism that throws me anxiously into what I imagine to have been the squalor of my paternal grandfather's first years in New York. The apartments are on display, like artworks into which you can enter, and Pedro, one of the museum's "educators," guides a dozen visitors up the building's tenebrous stairs.

A total of seven thousand immigrants from twenty countries lived in this one tenement building between 1863, the year it was built, and 1935, when the landlord, too stretched to comply with a fire-proofing ordinance, turned everyone out. Afterward, a discount clothing store on the ground floor stored its excess merchandise in the cold rooms upstairs. In 1998, it had the undisturbed look of a nineteenth-century time capsule and was turned into a museum.

Pedro leads us into the reconfigured digs of Nathalia Gumpertz, a German-born single mother of four who moved into the building during the Panic of 1873, when businesses failed, the Stock Exchange temporarily closed, and unemployment rocketed. Tiny windowless rooms; an outhouse shared with customers of the bar downstairs. "The neighborhood was known as Kleindeutschland back then," Pedro informs us. "It had the fifth largest concentration of German speakers in the world."

By 1890, East Europeans had overrun Kleindeutschland, and the Lower East Side was the most densely populated neighborhood in America. Twenty years later, my immigrant grandfather hit these streets, "a shtetl nobody," as he called himself, fifteen years of age, patching discarded trash cans and selling them to slum landlords about town. He bounced from place to place, sleeping where he could, until he was married and moved into a cold-water tenement a few blocks from Orchard Street, on Grand. "Mrs. Gumpertz's great-great-grandson was killed in the World Trade Center," says Pedro, showing us the picture of a dark-eyed middle-aged man.

Pedro ushers us in to the carefully assembled apartment of Harris and Jenny Levine, who lived in their own sweatshop. Everything is organized in its joyless way for work: flat irons on a coal stove, piles of dress sleeves waiting to be basted. A steel bucket with a blanket set in it is where the newborn baby was kept. The single stained bed is no more than a place to collapse. Peeled layers of pasteboard, enamel, and linoleum on the floor give it the look of a trampled collage.

Leaving the museum and walking around the corner, I am confronted with a luxury condominium tower with blue pixilated windows like so many sparkling computer screens. The Lower East Side is one of the four most lucrative neighborhoods in the U.S. in which to buy real estate, with a price appreciation of 125 percent during the past two years.*

I pass the lopsided former tenement on Grand Street where my grandparents brought up their four children. It's spruced up now as a one-family home. I picture my Uncle Ellie in those rooms. Seven years older than my father, he bore the mark of those harsh times in a way that my father, more confident and American, did not. Instead of joining the family scrap-metal business, Ellie worked as a crane operator, sliding about in his perch near the skylights of one warehouse or another like a demon in a flying cage. Even near death he was a seething heap of a man, six foot three, his outsized face lit with shattered capillaries and veins.

In 1983, at my father's request, I accompanied Ellie to the hospital emergency room. "I can't get myself to do it, Michael. He's my only brother." When Ellie was settled in his room, I helped him put on the standard hospital gown. "Where's Bernie?" he wanted to know, referring to my father. "Why isn't he here?"

As I was hanging up his pants, an enormous wad of money tumbled to the floor. Ellie insisted that I count it: $493 in singles and fives. "Keep it," he said. The bills were almost untouchable—Ellie had been incontinent—yet without hesitation I stuffed them, reeking and soiled, in my pockets.

I returned to my apartment on the Lower East Side, in a public housing project with a concrete playground that had replaced dozens of razed tenements. Improved living for the poor. I laid out Ellie's money, with all its sordid, scavenger power. My need for it was a mockery of my attempts

*Prices calculated from September 2004 to September 2006.

to transcend what I regarded as my family's grasping, immigrant-minded ways. Yet in a crisscross of logic, my very desire for the money drove me to hand it over to my father. As a grown man my father sometimes came home from the family's scrap-metal yard with blood dribbling out of the corner of his mouth where my grandfather had slugged him. They fought over the business that had lifted them out of the slums. Was it because it had been so scarce that money brought its new version of misery?

After drying the bills on a clothesline in my bathroom, I invited my father to come over. "Ellie gave me something for you," I told him. He had never visited me there, and I tried to imagine what my life in that building would look like to him. Two of the three elevators were out of order, and he had to wait fifteen minutes to ride up to my apartment on the nineteenth floor. Walking down the hall, he glimpsed the interior of my Chinese neighbors' place, their door ajar, as usual, ten or more restaurant workers lying side by side on red blankets across the floor.

Maintaining my illusion of purity, I handed him Ellie's money, folded neatly in a plastic bag.

He took it and left. Or so I thought—until I found it on the little table by the door. It was just enough to pay a month's rent.

Workroom

I HAVE A WORKROOM in the West Village, a boxy space where I have been writing, on and off, for the past twenty-five years. The rent is low, thanks to the generosity of a philanthropic foundation that purchased the building in the 1960s with the idea of supplying affordable studio space to artists. Officially, no one is permitted to live in the building, although through the years a few of us have surreptitiously camped out in our studios while waiting for hard times to blow over.

Previously, the building had been the Bell Telephone Company's research center. The transistor was invented here. But when the inventors cleared out and the artists moved in, an obscure inertia seemed to settle over the place. It was as if it existed in a reality of its own, at odds with the city to which it barely seemed to belong. When Manhattan roared, life in our building seemed to decelerate even further.

Although my workroom faces the Hudson, for years my view of the river was obstructed by an elevated highway that rose exactly to the height of my window on the second floor. The traffic made my walls tremble, until a loaded dump truck plunged through a pothole, and the highway, deemed excessively dangerous, was closed for good. New Yorkers immediately claimed the condemned road as a waterfront promenade.

I was giving Spanish lessons in my studio at around that time, and my best student was a nude dancer at one of dozens of gay bars that sprang to life each evening along our stretch of West Street. He sent several friends to me, and for a time I had a reasonable business greasing the wheels of conversation between Spanish- and English-speaking cruisers. At night, I would occasionally spot some of my students among the swarm of men who spilled out of the bars onto the street, dancing and humping with beer bottles held aloft. From the barred windows of the Men's House of Detention next door the prisoners watched the carousing with varying degrees of excitement, sending out a constant stream of curses and threats.

A short while later, the elevated highway was razed. My father complained that he had been shut out from acquiring the dismantled support beams for his scrap-metal yard, but to me it was like being delivered from a state of semi-blindness: suddenly I could see across the river to New Jersey's riotous petrochemical sunsets.

By the late 1980s, the House of Detention had been converted into luxury apartments, nightlife on West Street was decimated by AIDS, and my landlady, Dora, always cranky, had become almost impossible to deal with. Dora had grown up on the Gulf Coast of Louisiana, "a mess of mixed blood," she called herself—Cajun, African, Seminole Indian, Anglo-Saxon. In New York, she had traded her southern accent for the theatrical pitch of a 1950s Greenwich Village avant-gardist, and had a brief career as a soap opera actress. Dora's husband used the room as a painting studio and I have been subletting from her since he died.

Though she has little money and could easily get much more for the space, she charges me the same low rent that she pays. In return, she treats me as the son she never had, demanding deference while berating me for my boorishly insensitive behavior. She insists on criticizing my work, patronizes me with pep talks, and complains to her friends that, like her husband, I will never be sufficiently successful. She once threatened to evict me if I didn't try my hand at crime stories.

She still regards herself as a beauty, alluding on occasion to "gentlemen half my age" who are plotting to seduce her. Recently, it was a man she met while visiting Louisiana. Would I read his novel with an eye toward finding him an agent? It was called *America's Guts*. In a climactic scene, the hero, a colonel in the U.S. Marines, dumps a cargo planeful of hog's guts on an insurgent Muslim village.

Some time ago, I decided to work at home for a while. With Dora's consent, I offered the room to a young woman named Chloe, who was recommended by a friend.

On the phone, Chloe declares the place "a godsend, too good to be true." She is working on a novel and is eager to have the studio on any terms, even for a limited amount of time. When she sees it, however, she seems less enthusiastic. The place looks shabby, I think, a nondescript box, unnecessarily bare. I figure that I have spent more than 50,000 hours in this room and wonder aloud if the products of those hours—

from a first novel brought to an end because I couldn't bear to revise it anymore, to the voice-over narration for a television program about golf—have configured themselves into a single repellent mass.

I warn Chloe of Dora's eccentricities, then grow nostalgic for the garbage scows that used to float like clockwork past my window on their way to the landfill on Staten Island, before the landfill closed down. I remember Alexander Trocchi's description, in his novel *Cain's Book*, of working a scow along this stretch of the Hudson, looking at Manhattan "like a little mirage in which one isn't involved."

Chloe listens politely, straining to understand. She is youthful and optimistic, with a degree from an expensive university writing program. She worked as an assistant at a famous magazine, she tells me, and has contributed articles to others just as well known. She recites her credentials in the way of one who approaches writing as if it were a rational, upwardly mobile career.

I give her a tour of the communal bathroom. "I've seen worse," Chloe says gamely. One of my neighbors is in there, talking lazily on his cell phone while washing his hash-encrusted hookah.

Then I take her down the hall to meet Joe, the abstract expressionist painter, stocky and energetic at eighty-seven years of age. Delighted at the visit, Joe introduces himself as "the most famous unknown artist in America." A Maria Callas LP is playing scratchily on the phonograph and an avalanche of Joe's cheerful paintings are propped along the walls. He gravely informs her that his weakness for intellectual women ruined his career. "I should have gone to bed with Frank O'Hara when he came on to me at the Cedar Tavern."

Chloe promises to be in touch tomorrow, but a week passes without a word. Her silence stings me. I feel jilted, stood up. I try to see the building through her eyes: pot-heads and old men hiding away in their rooms. Finally, she sends me an email. "Your space is truly special. I wish for both of us that it was the one."

That evening Dora phones. There has been a minor fire in the building, just smoke, no flames, but firemen broke into our room to make sure that nothing was smoldering in the walls. "Management put a padlock on the door. Come over when you want to pick up the key."

I stop by her apartment, crowded with her husband's Kokoschka-inspired paintings, including a portrait of Dora as a young woman that captures her sharp features and un-compromising glare. "I can't bear to throw them out," she says of the paintings, "but no one wants to buy them. Take note for your own future, Michael. If only my husband had paid closer attention to his career."

My workroom looks more forlorn than ever, with the door hanging off its hinges, the molding ripped out, and several holes chopped in the sheetrock walls. I phone Dora to describe the damage. After a pause, she says: "Do stay on. You know as well as I do that you can't leave now." Dora is right. Chances are I'll be back in my room by spring, counting the hours.

SEVERAL YEARS AGO I began to chronicle my daily commute on the number 1 train, from the 110th Street subway station on Manhattan's Upper West Side to the 14th Street station in Greenwich Village. It was a joke I played on myself, an attempt to make a virtue of the fact that I hadn't ventured more than fifty miles from New York City in almost a decade.

"Notes of an Anti-Traveler," I called it, trying to give a literary burnish to the rut I was in. "9.49 a.m. Twenty-six people on the downtown platform. Rain spilling on to the tracks from a scabrous-looking iron girder. What appears to be a large black clam is sitting in a rising puddle near the third rail. I look harder. It's a cell phone."

Occasionally I subjected myself to unnecessary hardship for the sake of research, such as remaining in a subway car with a strong-smelling homeless woman after everyone else had abandoned it. "Hers was a cultivated stench, a kind of sheathing that protects her from being assaulted when she sleeps. By the time we reach Lincoln Center I am almost accustomed to the smell." At 59th Street a man in a Burberry coat boarded the car, sat down with a polite nod, and began reading his newspaper, oblivious to her, and me.

Six months of note-taking confirmed what I already knew: a successful commute is one in which nothing unusual happens. Most people regard with distaste the possibility of adventure that comes with being in a closed capsule crowded with strangers. If something out of the ordinary occurs, commuters ignore it in the hope that it will soon end. I was seeing things from another angle: unable to break out of the monotony of my days, I focused with greater intensity on it, in the hope that there was more to the monotony than I had suspected.

My most interesting encounter was with a singer with small hands from Nicaragua who played boleros for donations at various subway stations on a miniature guitar. We ran into each other once or twice a month, always happy for each other's company. He was a tenor, with a deep arresting voice that had a cultivated catch to it that was like a cry. He worked on a folding stool, like a classical guitarist, with his legs slightly apart, his back held straight, and the butt of the instrument resting on his right thigh.

I worried about him after not seeing him for a couple of months. When he reappeared, he explained that he had "lost the spirit. I was pushing too hard. Higher volume, louder voice, but I couldn't make myself heard." He told me he had been reading a book. "Una novela. Maybe you know it. Don Quijote de la Mancha."

I thought he was pulling my leg, but he seemed sincere, as if he had just stumbled across the book, or maybe he believed that because I was a gringo I would be unfamiliar with it.

"What do you think it's about?" he asked. When I started to answer, he cut me off. "No, no. You've got it wrong. It's about a man who hates the present, just as I do. But he doesn't want to hate, because it poisons you to hate, so he creates a way not to, but it's a fantasía that makes him crazy."

The seven-block walk from the 14th Street subway to my workroom was another leg of the commute—and equally uneventful. My theory was that, because I never varied my route, I had become as habituated to the street as the street was to me. Together we imposed an expectation of sameness on each other that we unfailingly fulfilled. Whenever I changed routes, my theory was proved to be true. I walked on West 11th Street instead of Bank Street, and a man walking in the opposite direction rammed his shoulder into me, feigning an accidental collision. Out of his pocket fell a pint bottle of vodka, which shattered on the pavement. "Look what you did," he shouted. "Give me money for another bottle!" Ascertaining that the bottle had been filled with water, I refused, and he punched me in the face and scurried off. The following day I returned to my old route.

I had forgotten about these notes and the modest incidents they describe, until a few days ago when I picked up an anti-travelogue by Julio Cortázar and his wife Carol Dunlop: *Autonauts of the Cosmoroute: A Timeless Voyage from Paris to Marseilles*. In May 1982, the couple left Paris for Marseilles in their Volkswagen camper, normally a ten-hour drive. They set themselves two rules: never to exit the autoroute, and to stop at every one of the sixty-five rest areas along the way, at the rate of two a day, "with the obvious obligation of sleeping in the second one."

The trip took thirty-three days. Unlike my commuting, their expedition was senseless, and optimistically opposed to the world as it is. It was just a game, devoid of underlying intentions, they claimed, an exercise in monotony. By the fifth day, they were surprised to discover that their routine felt natural. The rest areas seemed as diverse as different cities, even though some were no more than a tongue of asphalt next to the freeway. Cortázar and Dunlop were living with a happy intensity that came from being still while everyone around them was moving at maximum speed.

As an experiment, I planted myself on the corner of 109th Street and Amsterdam Avenue for several hours without moving. It was Friday, half past four, raining softly, automobile traffic moving north toward Harlem. Dozens of people went into the deli on the corner, emerging with scratch-off lottery tickets, which they rubbed, then dropped on the ground.

After an hour, the pavement around me was covered with hundreds of discarded tickets, their silver borders glistening in the rain. A father rushed by with twin three-year-old daughters, each grasping one of his hands, and running to keep up. One of the girls lost her sneaker while crossing the street, and the father kicked it onto the sidewalk so it wouldn't be crushed by a car. Behind me, a ten-dollar drug deal went down. A Senior Care ambulance pulled up in front of the building on the corner. A smiling woman was unstrapped from a gurney, fastened into a wheelchair, and carried by two attendants into her building, returning home.

By eight o'clock, I felt a pleasant empty peacefulness that overcame my desire to get out of the rain or move on.

13

"*REMEMBER WHAT I'M SAYING*, Michael: more important than what you do for a living is who you do it for. Are you slaving for another man's fortune? Or can you hold your head up and call yourself your own boss?"

That was my grandfather Louie's credo, drummed into me as a boy. He refused to allow that there was an employee on earth who wasn't tyrannized by the urge to murder the man who paid him.

"These high rollers you see with their big-shot salaries? Believe me, what they buy with their money tastes foul."

When I turned eleven, Louie demanded to know how I intended to earn my keep. And how soon did I plan on starting? His own childhood seemed like something out of the pages of Saul Bellow's *The Adventures of Augie March*. He arrived alone in Manhattan from the Ukraine at the age of fifteen—one of the "unfinished people," as the writer Ruth

Gay called the gang of adolescent immigrants from turn-of-the-twentieth-century Eastern Europe: too old to slough off the Old Country completely, but young enough to be American-formed. His first New York job was as a street peddler. He welded trash cans in a basement on Grand Street, then piled them onto a pushcart, and sold them to slumlords in Little Italy and the Lower East Side. "First-rate receptacles, Michael. No partner. No boss."

Partly inspired by Louie, I now realize, I left home as a teenager and dropped out of school. In retrospect, the move seems rash, but I was sold on the idea that it was a shortcut to becoming a writer. If only Louie had known how to tell a story, I thought.

My mother accused me of squandering the benefits of my grandfather's immigrant "sacrifice," which after his death had taken on an almost-sacred aura. As I saw it, the real sacrifice was on the part of those who had to toe the line and forswear a free-style existence. "First to knock, first admitted," in Saul Bellow's words. "Sometimes an innocent knock, sometimes a not so innocent."

Four or five years later, broke and without a job, I was working as a street peddler myself. I specialized in cosmetics— eye pencils, compacts, lip gloss, and the like. My supplier operated out of a three-room apartment above a wig shop in Brooklyn. The place was packed from floor to ceiling with knockoffs designed to look as if they had been manufactured by Helena Rubinstein and Lancôme. He sold them for a buck apiece. "Tell your customers they're hot," he advised me when I inquired what to do if questioned about the legal status of my wares. "It'll make them think they're getting a bargain."

Manhattan was off-limits to newcomers. On a tip from a Chilean immigrant called Lucho, I set my sights on Fordham Road, a shopping district in the Bronx. Lucho took it upon himself to teach me the ropes. "If you're not careful, street-vending is just another way of starving." He admired my makeup kits, which were improbably handsome considering how little they cost: oyster-shell compacts filled with blush and mascara, and brushes with which to apply them. Lucho sold golden sticks of fried sugary dough from a plastic milk crate. Because of what he called our "complementary products," he suggested we work in tandem. *"Belleza y comida."* Beauty and food.

He had staked out a stretch of pavement in front of a women's department store on the east side of Fordham Road. It was right under the elevated train tracks. Lucho knew the security guard at the store. For a small payoff, he'd refrain from chasing us away. I displayed my wares on an ironing board, decorated with an embroidered cloth. Lucho set up a few feet away with his bread sticks.

At mid-morning, the number 4 train thundered overhead, and the sunlight that had managed to seep through the tracks grew thick with steel dust. Lucho covered his bread with cellophane to protect it from the droppings of the pigeons nesting in the girders. An hour or so could pass without a sale. Between trains, the street felt thoughtful and still. And then, for no apparent reason, I would be surrounded by women, chattering in Spanish, nibbling on Lucho's dough while contemplating themselves in the hand-mirrors I provided. "May I try the eye shadow?" "Do you have a darker shade of lipstick?" Taking their money, I would be reminded of Gorky's description of trapping songbirds for his grandmother to sell in town at the market. He was ashamed to put the birds in cages. "I preferred just watching them. But my passion for trapping and the desire to earn money overcame my feeling of regret."

I began by charging $3.50 for a compact, but Lucho pointed out that the price made buyers suspicious, so I raised it to five bucks and business picked up. I grew attached to my customers and, not wanting to deceive them, I admitted that my cosmetics were counterfeit. Most appeared not to care. "I like the impression it makes when I take it out of my bag," one told me.

At nightfall, Lucho would feed his unsold bread to the pigeons. Sometimes we split a half-pint of vodka. He showed me his Dali-inspired drawings, terrifying images that he claimed came directly from his dreams. He was saving money to rent a stall in one of Fordham Road's discount outlets where he could sell sunglasses, cheap toys, and, perhaps, his drawings.

My most profitable day was the Saturday before Easter. To my surprise, Lucho didn't show up. As I was preparing to leave, three teenagers robbed me of goods and cash. The following week Lucho was nowhere to be found. I never discovered whether he was involved in what had happened. The security guard at the department store informed me that he wouldn't be able to protect me any longer, and my career as a street vendor ended.

Visiting Fordham Road now, I find it almost unchanged. "For sale!" cries a peddler wheeling a brand-new bicycle along the sidewalk. In my old spot in front of the department store, a man is selling underwear and bootleg DVDs. He tells me of his elaborate scheme to build an orphanage in Liberia, where he was born. "I'll show American executives the beautiful thing I've done and they'll give me money."

The main thing is to be your own boss.

Tycoon

THE OTHER DAY I came across something I had scribbled in an old notebook: "Reverend Ike, wearing gold, tells his broke congregants that money is an article of faith. Like God."

It was 1978. I was making my living moving furniture in a used van with a hired helper. Between jobs I looked after my two-year-old son and worked on my novel. On the subway, I had been handed a flyer advertising one of Reverend Ike's inspirational talks about prosperity. The only obstacle to wealth, preached the reverend, is "your poor person's state of mind." I studied Ike's neon smile, crumpled the flyer into a ball and threw it in the garbage.

I had just lost five thousand dollars in the stock market. I had made the investment, my first, with the hope that from its return I would be able to buy more time for my novel, on which I had already spent four years. Where money is concerned, however, hope is counterproductive. Skepticism would have been a more useful attitude. "Consider it an educational loss," said the broker who had sold me the security. "You can't know beans about the market until you've been burned."

Two years later, I sold the novel, only to have its publication canceled when the publishing company changed corporate hands and my editor was fired. This confirmed my growing belief that my literary efforts were a mockery of the basic relationship between money and labor—I was working for virtually nothing.

The stock market, of course, distorts that relationship in the opposite way. Buying shares in a company turns you into an economic parasite. You are the silent partner, hidden, inert. Your money is the productive one, not you. I was in the absurd position of working hard for no pay, while trying to make money by not working. My so-called publisher's new corporate parent, I noticed, was listed on the New York Stock Exchange.

I immediately began raising a stake for another foray into the market—"discretionary capital," the financial advisers call it. I felt like Saul Bellow's character Wilky, in *Seize the Day*, who has persisted in his quest to be an actor just long enough to make himself unfit for the more lucrative professions. Wilky falls under the spell of a fast talker called Tamkin. Like Reverend Ike, Tamkin sees prosperity in strictly psychological terms: it's all a question of self-confidence and nerve. He claims to have cracked the "guilt-aggression cycle" that is behind the market's ups and downs. Investing, he says, "is filled with hostile feeling and lust. People come to the market to kill. They say, 'I'm going to make a killing.' Only they haven't got the genuine courage to kill, and they erect a symbol to it. The money."

Tamkin takes Wilky to a brokerage office where gnomic old men seem to be weaving gold from thin air. Following Tamkin's advice, Wilky bets his entire savings on lard, and loses.

Playing the market may be the respectable cousin of gambling, but for me there are no thrills in the game. After getting burned the first time out, I have become like the plodding card counter you sometimes see at the casino blackjack table, methodically trying to tilt the odds in his favor. I have discovered that I have an improbable facility for assessing gross profit margins, debt-to-asset ratios, and lurking areas of growth in a company's revenue stream. This activity, I tell myself, brings out a level-headedness that is in short supply in other areas of my life. However, for years I have kept it a secret, fearing that it somehow discredits me as a writer. In some circles it would be regarded as a point of social and political shame. I occasionally wonder if I missed my true calling, as a stock analyst poring over corporate reports in the back office of some Wall Street firm.

Unfortunately, when my analysis is accurate, my timing usually isn't. After the collapse of the Mexican peso in 1994, I threw everything I had into Telmex, the Mexican telephone monopoly, betting that the U.S. Treasury would come to the rescue. The peso would stabilize, I figured, and shares of Telmex would rise.

It was a bold move, but I didn't have the stomach for it; I lacked Tamkin's aggressive impulse toward risk. After scouring the financial papers each morning for information that might shed light on my investment, I would finally sit down to work. I would write a few sentences, go over to the local bar, and drink bourbon while gazing at the stock ticker that ran along the bottom of a silent television screen. After a couple of months, I sold Telmex in order to be able to think straight again.

During the entire next year, I watched the shares I no longer owned dramatically increase in value.

Finding myself in Lower Manhattan, I wander over to the Stock Exchange, a Greek Revival mass whose Corinthian columns are wreathed in frosted light for Hanukkah and Christmas. A giant menorah hangs over the entrance where shivering traders gather to smoke. Six brightly painted nutcracker soldiers stand guard on the balconies, while below, in front of the barricades, are the real guards, gray-faced and bored.

I am studying the colossal sculpture in the pediment—Integrity with wings in her skull protecting the commercial endeavors of Man—when one of the guards approaches, wanting to know what I am writing in my notebook. Dissatisfied with my answer, he demands to see identification, then returns to his post with a warning stare.

The incident reminds me of the day, in 1968, when our high school history teacher canceled class to lead us down to an anti–Vietnam War demonstration at the Exchange. "You're looking at the vault in which the industrial-military complex throbs," announced our teacher. But it's also like a department store, I thought, where the country's entire productive capacity is for sale. As I marched miserably in the cold, a policeman whacked me in the hams with his billy club. "You're too close to the building!" he barked. Hard not to loathe such a place. But the instant I sank my money into the market, the revolutionary inside me retreated.

A survey in 2003 found that nearly 20 percent of Americans believe they are among the wealthiest 1 percent. Another 30 percent are convinced they will get there before long. I credit myself with not having yet descended to this level of delusion, but I know really it's just my poor person's state of mind.

A Falsely Young Man

15

THE RECENT COLLAPSE of stock prices has put me in mind of another credit scam: the Stavisky affair in France in 1934. From the city of Bayonne's municipal pawnshops, Serge Alexandre Stavisky, the former manager of a nightclub and a tinned-soup factory, floated hundreds of millions of francs worth of bonds. The bonds, as Janet Flanner explained in her Letter from Paris column in the *New Yorker*, were "bought up by life-insurance companies, counseled by the Minister of Colonies, who was counseled by the Minister of Commerce, who was counseled by the mayor of Bayonne, who was counseled by the little manager of the hockshop, who was counseled by Stavisky."

The value of the bonds was backed by what Stavisky claimed were the emeralds of the former empress of Germany— "fifteen million francs worth of spinach colored glass." The losses spread throughout France, caused the resignations of two prime ministers, provoked a failed military coup, and ended with fourteen deaths after a riot of more than 100,000 people on the Boulevard Saint-Germain.

I feel as if I am getting a reasonably accurate portrait of the less than circumspect financiers at Lehman Brothers and AIG, when Flanner describes Stavisky as a staid, methodical deviser of fraudulent financial instruments, whose "table jokes fell flat, and who, though forced for business reasons to have mistresses, loved only his wife." On the run after his pyramid scheme crumbled, the official story is that Stavisky committed suicide, though circumstances suggest that he was killed by the police in order to keep him from implicating the ministers and financiers who had helped his scam grow from a provincial embezzlement to a national crisis. According to Flanner, part of the public's shock when the Stavisky scandal broke came from the fact that no one had ever heard of him before, "except the judges, lawyers, political mandarins and detectives who had been stretching the jailbird's provisional liberty for the last six years."

Colette, who was his neighbor at Claridge's Hotel, called him "a falsely young man," whose "delicate complexion demanded constant care." His final gentle letter to his wife begged her to raise their two children "in the sentiments of honor and probity, and when they reach the ungrateful age of fifteen to watch over their associations."

Recently, as the cascade of phony "mortgage swaps" and "derivatives" poured out of their hiding places, I received a call from a friend I'll call Peter, the closest person to the spirit of Stavisky I know.

Peter and I grew up together in Rockaway. When he was still in his early twenties, he acquired a mail-order law degree from a college I'd never heard of in Las Vegas. His specialty was tax law, but his real talent was as a fixer, or, as he put it, an ability to "smooth matters over at the last minute." His clients were bar owners, hardware retailers, small-time land-lords, and restaurateurs who relied on Peter to take care of their most intractable conflicts with the Internal Revenue Service.

He differed most from Stavisky and other world-class con men in his refusal—or inability—to think of money abstractly. As a capitalist, he operated strictly on the street level, con-verting the money he made as a tax adviser into a mini-fleet of taxi cabs, a dozen hot dog and falafel carts, a business that installed automobile alarms, and a share in a funeral home on Flatbush Avenue in Brooklyn. The secret to his success, he said, was that he "thought small and acted big." He hated the stock market, and had never owned a publicly traded security in his life. "When you give your money to strangers, don't expect to see returns."

I was surprised to hear from Peter, since we spoke infre-quently. On the phone he sounded tense. "Would you mind coming over to my place? It would be a relief to see an old friend for a change."

Rockaway is a delicate, weather-battered peninsula in Queens, the final stop on the A train and the easternmost part of New York City. I walked the fifteen blocks from the sub-way to Peter's house, enjoying the abandoned resort-town feeling that invariably comes over Rockaway in the fall, after the mass of day-trippers from Manhattan and Brooklyn have stopped coming to its beaches.

Peter's house, which he grew up in, an only child, was reassuringly unchanged. His parents were a quiet, anxious, pessimistic couple, whom Peter pitied and adored. They had owned a modest dry-cleaning establishment in the neighborhood. When they were in their fifties, beset with various health problems that Peter reasonably blamed on the chemicals they were exposed to in the store, he bought them a condominium in Florida, a welcome early retirement that Peter paid for without a hint of resentment.

He let me into the house, sat me down in the kitchen where his father used to tally up his pink customer receipts, and explained the reason for his agitation. In an attempt to bypass inheritance tax, an elderly client had transferred all of his assets to his son. A few months after the transfer, however, the son had a heart attack and died. The money reverted back to the old man, minus a 55 percent tax bite on a portfolio that was already disintegrating in the stock market decline.

Peter tried to set matters straight with his contact at the IRS, but he didn't know that the agent had recently been caught accepting a bribe from someone else, and that, as part of a deal for leniency he struck with his employers, he was taping their meeting. "I can handle being disbarred, and even the twenty-two months in a federal prison I'm going to get after I plea-bargain next week. But I told my client the bribe would cost 115 grand, and there I am on tape offering twenty-five. My credibility is shot."

I reminded him of the summer I drove one of his cabs. It was 1975. In the previous seventeen months the real value of the New York Stock Exchange had fallen by more than half. On 11th Avenue, while I was standing at a red light, a man slid into the front seat and aimed a gun at me. Although it was August, he was wearing a woolen overcoat, and shivering— a junkie in need of a fix.

Under normal circumstances, I would have handed over my money without protest, but Peter had installed a small safe under the seat, where I was to deposit the money from each fare, keeping only enough for change. The key was in Peter's garage. I tried to explain this to the junkie but he seemed too distressed to make sense of it, so I rolled to the next red light, jumped out of the cab and ran off. By the time the light turned green, the junkie was in the driver's seat, heading uptown. When the cab was found a couple of days later, it had been stripped bare and set on fire.

"Did you make out okay?" Peter asked me at the time, implying that I had profited in some way from the incident, or perhaps had invented the story of the junkie and torched the cab myself. "You couldn't bear my getting rich, while you were a grunt making thirty bucks a night driving my car."

We didn't speak for twenty years after that. Now he told me that I had misunderstood him. He hadn't meant to insult me. "On the contrary, I thought the better of you for it. It showed you had some imagination."

16

IN THE EARLY 1980S, cured by my first novel of any illusions I'd had about the glories of self-expression, I decided to approach writing as just another part-time venture, like selling cosmetics or driving a cab. When a friend recommended me to a former Manhattan restaurateur who sought a ghostwriter for her "tell-all memoir," I leapt at the job. My employer, a middle-aged Parisian with gold clamshell earrings and pulled-back blond hair, had been the proprietor, with her ex-husband, of a four-star restaurant on the Upper East Side. "Henry Kissinger was one of our regular diners. So was Leonard Bernstein. Beverly Sills. They all came, and not only for the food. For the atmosphere. The discretion." At the height of its popularity the restaurant closed down, owing to an almost generic scandal involving tax evasion and the increasing appetite of the would-be memoirist's husband for Armagnac and cocaine.

We agreed I would be paid by the hour. Each morning at ten, I would arrive with my legal pad at her small, over-furnished apartment in a white-brick high rise on Third Avenue. "My gilded slum," she called it. With the imperiousness of the hostess whose welcoming embrace had once conferred on its recipients instant social prestige, she assured me that her agent, Swifty Lazar, was eagerly awaiting "the fruits of our labor." Lazar had been another regular diner at her restaurant; he planned, she said, to present her memoir "to all the best publishers" at an auction.

After two days, I realized that it would be impossible to extract from her a coherent narrative. She overestimated the dramatic value of her downfall and seemed unwilling to give up the air of one whose invitation to the grand ball had been unfairly rescinded. It was her bookkeeping, in part, that led to the restaurant's demise. Yet her disappointments had a hidden complexity. In the midst of a painful recollection, she would interrupt herself with a shiver and turn away as if she had spotted something revolting out of the corner of her eye.

At the end of a week, Swifty Lazar had been forgotten; it was obvious that nothing would come of our conversations. In need of the money, however, I let the job drag on. At least I was less expensive than a psychoanalyst, I argued to myself, as I jotted down notes on my pad with an air of sympathetic detachment. My biggest letdown was the food. I had hoped to be the beneficiary of a few memorable meals, but the husband had been the chef, and he was serving eighteen months in jail. My employer seemed content with grilled cheese sandwiches wrapped in tin foil from the coffee shop down the street.

Since then I've had numerous jobs as a writer-for-hire, like a subcontractor who works on various parts of a house, without ever building one from start to finish himself. Lately, I've grown suspicious of my ability to manufacture sincerity, to write with apparent conviction about that in which I have no real interest, and I have repeatedly resolved to give up such employment. However, when Zebra Davis phones with what he describes as "the perfect offer," I agree to meet with him and learn more.

I walk downtown to the Chelsea Hotel on West 23rd Street where Zebra—he gave himself the name during his brief career as a performance artist in the 1970s—is currently living. The Chelsea wears its literary history like derelict clothes. In one of its rooms Arthur Miller wrote *A View from the Bridge* and *After the Fall*. Dylan Thomas was staying here when he drank himself to death at the White Horse Tavern. Virgil Thomson, James Schuyler, Brendan Behan, Thomas Wolfe— the commemorative plaques are stacked one atop another on either side of the front entrance.

I wait in the lobby, among the paintings that former tenants exchanged for their rooms and the cockroach traps discreetly placed in the corners. Finally, Zebra comes down in a sleeveless T-shirt with occult tattoos on his weight-lifter's arms. The last thing I wrote for him was a downmarket program for late-night cable television entitled "Heroic Dogs."

Zebra proudly shows me a copy of his latest volume of self-published poems: *Hieronymus Bosch Eats Breakfast at McDonald's.* "This is what really matters to me," he says. "The rest is crap. A necessary evil. I tell you this, Michael, because I know you understand." The author's photo is an extreme close-up of

Zebra's teeth and gums, a homage, he explains, to his late father, who was a dentist.

Over lunch at Burritoville, a fast-food joint near the hotel, Zebra tells me about the job: the story of golf during the past one hundred years. The budget is tight. The visuals will consist of stock footage and newsreel. "This project depends on the writing, Michael. Two hours of voice-over narration." He instructs me to connect, whenever possible, great moments in golf with important historical events. For added drama, I'm to emphasize the rivalry between American and British players, especially in the early years of the twentieth century. "The Americans come out on top, of course." The program will be broadcast on a cable sports channel. It is to be called "The Game that Defined a Century."

As I set to work, a familiar dullness comes over me— the dullness of empty language. "Golf. Simple. Majestic. Timeless," I begin. "Imagine a rabbit hole in the wild Scottish grass. Striking a stone with his stick, a solitary walker aims for the hole." Later: "1922. Americans invent the potato chip. Walter Hagen hauls his golf bag across the pond to capture the British Open." Then: "1945. Allied troops march triumphantly through Europe. And Byron Nelson mounts a march of his own: eleven consecutive victories on the PGA tour." Augusta National golf club, where the Masters is played, is "Bobby Jones's masterpiece, a sonnet of landscape architecture."

I complete the script and send it off to Zebra. A week later he phones. An executive at the network has complimented my "intimate feeling for the game." Would I be available to play a round with him at the Westchester Country Club next Thursday? I confess to Zebra that I have never played golf, except for a few holes of miniature golf on Kings Highway in Brooklyn when I was a boy.

"We'll tell him you're sick," says Zebra without skipping a beat. "Something highly contagious."

TO WRITE SUCCESSFULLY for the movies you have to live in Los Angeles, where the action is. That should be enough to disqualify me from pursuing a screenwriting career: I've only been to Los Angeles once, to attend the funeral of my maternal grandmother who spent her last years in a walled community for retirees that was so huge it had its own bus company. Nevertheless, I occasionally land work writing for the odd movie or television show here in New York.

These jobs are apt to be in the margins of the industry, where I've serviced aspiring directors, or older ones who have fallen from favor, millionaires who have lost their heads over some chimerical project, documentary filmmakers, and the like. I fell into this line of work when a producer with a checkered past bought a story of mine for hard cash, then paid me again to turn it into a screenplay. I was so grateful I made the greenhorn error of signing over the rights to him "in perpetuity." When I realized I'd been swindled, I did what I could to make sure my story was never filmed, hardly caring that I was sabotaging myself as well as the producer.

Subsequent jobs, when I find them, are, as my contracts state bluntly, "work-for-hire." Often I am merely ghostwriting. By giving up formal credit, I'm sure to be well liked by other members of "the creative team" (as we enjoy calling ourselves) and completely disrespected, since only a putz would renounce such a fundamental reward. Credit in the movie business is a kind of parallel coin. Without it you can't advance in the industry or even prove that you had anything to do with the glowing product on the screen. A writer I know was offered a small fortune to take his name off an original screenplay. The director couldn't bear to admit that the movie he'd made did not originate entirely in his own mind. My friend told him to go to hell. I know what I would have said.

My credit sacrifices have allowed me to maintain the facile superiority of one who has little at stake. You can't gain much if your name's not in lights, but you can't lose either. Sometimes this attitude catches up with me; I wonder if I'm trying to shield myself from the trials of competition, the heartache and paranoia that come with being in the fray. Lately, I've taken to accentuating my obscurity as a kind of identity in itself, a badge of honor. Sometimes I insist on it.

The money isn't especially good at this end of the business, but the work is relatively easy. The hardest part is having to pretend to care about plots and characters you'd be ashamed to have invented on your own, a costly insincerity when it spills over into other aspects of your working life (suddenly a character in the short story you're writing is "mid-thirties, athletic, withholding"). Another penalty is time wasted with the creative team fantasizing about famous actors who will fall over themselves for the chance to participate in our movie. The brightest luminaries are referred to by their first names—Uma, Marty, Sean—not out of pretentiousness, nor, it goes without saying, out of close acquaintance, but to bolster our spirits in the face of a harsh fact: success is a long shot.

Unusual for me, then, was a recent job on a movie with a bona-fide star in the lead role, a mini-studio behind its release, and a budget several times larger than any picture I had worked on previously. By the time I was hired, the movie had been shot, cut, and was all but ready for public consumption.

Vague dissatisfactions lingered, however, and I was asked to rewrite the voice-over narration that punctuated the action, the only aspect of the movie that could still be revised. The director interviewed me in a New York editing room where he agonized over his creation with an obsessiveness that was driving his assistants to despair. His work ethic made me feel cynical and lazy. But unrelenting toil was no help to him at this point. His microscopic examination of every frame had made it impossible for him to conceive of a fresh image or word.

I sympathized with his predicament and looked forward to what I assumed would be a generous pay day. I could not have been more wrong. The studio sensed a bomb in the making and was already cutting its losses. A tenacious infighter, the director had wrung a long series of concessions from them; hiring me, evidently, was the last straw. When I phoned LA to discuss the details of my employment, I was treated with a brusqueness that was difficult not to take to heart. "This walk-and-talk piece of shit is going to cost me my bonus!" the voice on the other end of the line bawled, before slamming down the receiver. They offered me a laughable fee, which of course I accepted.

I had ulterior motives as well: this director was going places. He possessed supernatural optimism, coercive charm, and a knowledge of pop culture comparable to a preacher's familiarity with Scripture. During a work lull one day, I pitched him a story I had lying around: a police reporter affects the outcome of the crimes he covers, then writes about them, hiding his involvement. "That's the plot of Superman," he said without hesitation. That I had not considered this similarity myself made me realize I was out of my league.

In due course, the movie was released. Opening-day reviews were bad. The protagonist was a dentist, and among the voice-over lines I wrote were these: "A man can lose a lot of things. He can lose his life. He can lose his soul. But the worst thing he can lose are his teeth." Quoting this, the *New York Times* said that unfortunately after twenty minutes the movie loses all three.

At the customary party for the crew that night, I was surprised when the bartender asked me to pay for my drink. Apparently the studio had pulled the plug even on this traditional courtesy. The director was on his fifth tequila when he gripped my shoulders and said: "Greenberg, they used your line to screw me."

I ended up in a corner talking with a screenwriter who happened to be at the party. He'd worked on at least fifty movies. One of them was a hit. But they took his credit away in arbitration.

18

THE IDEA, back in the late 1970s, was to make ready cash with no skills, no investment, as little expenditure of brain power as possible, and to do it without becoming a stick-up artist or otherwise breaking the law. The result was an exhausting progression of dead-end jobs, which included chauffeuring wealthy schoolchildren about in a limousine, and sorting mail for the U.S. Post Office on the graveyard shift near Grand Central Station. Honesty at the post office was regularly tested by the planting of twenty-dollar bills on the conveyer belt— a ploy that even the dope fiends, who had taken the job to swipe pharmaceutical samples addressed to doctors, knew not to fall for.

My goal was to avoid the psychological rut of "working for the Man." My status was low, but loyalty to employers wasn't required, allowing the illusion of independence that seemed of paramount importance. To my friends I explained that I was serving a literary apprenticeship, but a more powerful force was in operation: I couldn't bear the prospect of pinning myself to a "career." The joke was that I was willing to work harder than the next person to ensure that I didn't have one. To really achieve distinction, I believed, one's failure must be total.

Given these criteria, New York's restaurants were an obvious choice for employment. I prowled Fourteenth Street, where scores of agents in one-room offices competed for waiters, busboys, line cooks, and sudbusters—as dishwashers were called—in a row of low-rise buildings that have since been torn down.

Restaurant workers are the urban equivalent of field hands. About 40 percent are "undocumented aliens," and many of the rest are either rehab cases, runaways, or parolees. Wandering the halls with them, I found my way to an agent with a paper spike on her desk impaled with "leads." I told her I had waited tables at an upscale steakhouse in Boston, aware that my relatively fair complexion and native English made the lie easy to believe. She referred me to a posh cafe on East 44th Street, near the United Nations. "You'll be in the front of the house. Be sure to wear the appropriate clothes."

I didn't know yet that what is done well is invisible, and, having eaten at some decent restaurants, I assumed that waiting tables was as straightforward as it seemed. In a pinch, my fellow waiters would show me the ropes. But my lack of skill was apparent at once, and bitterly resented. I was shunned by the waiters, dissed by the busboys, and, when news of my charade spread to the kitchen, was openly cursed when I stepped in there.

One day, the maitre d' welcomed the head of a party of eight as "Mr. Ambassador," and led them to my station. My panic was palpable, destroying the area of protection that it is the waiter's job to draw around his service. The time came to open the wine. I was unfamiliar with the corkscrew, and the bottle of Mouton ended up between my legs as I struggled to yank out the cork. In an attempt to make light of my performance, I appealed to the ambassador's daughter, who was around my age. She turned away with her hands over her eyes.

I stepped down the ladder to a cavernous Midtown lunch place—triple-decker sandwiches, oversize burgers, broiled fluke, and chicken cacciatore. I thought my maiden shift went well, but the manager fired me for having lit a cigarette on the floor during a lull in service. When I pointed out that other waiters did the same, he said that a customer had complained about my "threatening" demeanor. "I can't expect my regulars to put up with this kind of vibration."

My final stop was a tiny falafel joint on MacDougal Street where one couldn't possibly scrape enough tips off the tables to survive. I left after two days, first to peddle fire alarms, then to teach Spanish, then to drive a cab.

I remember the day in the early 1980s, when, fed up with the drudgery to which I had sentenced myself, and aware that with two children at home it was too late to change course, I had followed a well-dressed man out of the subway, into a building, up the elevator, and all the way to the door of his office. A regular paycheck had become my version of paradise.

Jean-Paul

19

I AM AT A MIDTOWN ART GALLERY, at a friend's opening, when I spot Jean-Paul. I haven't seen him in almost fifteen years and I am surprised at how dwindled he looks in his blue smock and neglected five-day beard. I immediately recall the unpleasant circumstances under which we parted ways, but Jean-Paul disarms me with a joyous embrace, followed by news of his recent heart surgery which he claims has turned him into a new man. "They warn you about post-surgery depression," he says, "but I'm humming like an overhauled car."

Jean-Paul is an independent film producer with his share of hard-luck stories about missed blockbusters that would have put him in the money for life. When we met, he was involved in the making of a philosophical road movie whose script I admired. He was eager to buy the film rights to a story of mine and I was just as eager to sell them. My writing wasn't earning a dime and I was in the midst of cobbling together enough money for the down payment on a New York City taxi. Jean-Paul's offer felt like a last-minute pardon.

My story was "high concept," in the parlance of the business, which, Jean-Paul informed me, greatly increased its chances of being filmed. A disgraced big city journalist returns to his home town, where he lands a job as crime reporter on the local rag. He ends up writing about burglaries that he himself commits, turns his burglar into an idealized figure, and then uses this figure to seduce the woman who had rejected him as a younger man. Four writers took a crack at the screenplay, myself included. The challenge was to make the reporter desperate enough to go to all this trouble for a girl. When we had what we thought was a satisfactory script, Jean-Paul made the rounds of the studios. In what proved to be a typical response, one executive told him: "The kind of people who will relate to this lunatic you can count on one hand."

During this period I was a regular dinner guest at Jean-Paul's duplex in the West Village. How he paid for his luxurious existence was a mystery. His upbringing in a grim Parisian suburb sounded like something out of a novel by Céline. He dropped vague hints about his powerful social contacts, complaining that they had to be nurtured and propitiated like gods. Many of his friends had famous parents, yet seemed at loose ends themselves. There were always astrologers, palm readers, and self-proclaimed psychics in Jean-Paul's house. His wife, Stephanie, was a numerologist. She excitedly informed me that I was "an eleven, a master number." With a great air of significance, she pondered the "numerical vibrancy" of my name. One night she announced to the dinner table that although I had "a lot of potential," I was "impractical, undisciplined, destined to blow it."

About a month later, Jean-Paul set me up with a fashion photographer whose ambition was to direct "a grand love story," as he described it, a kind of update of *Funny Face* set in the world of haute couture. I was hired to write the script, which was subject at all times to the would-be director's approval.

I felt like a seasonal farmhand, allowed to stay in the bunkhouse until the crops were in the ground. Afterward, I was expected to disappear. This suited me just fine. The film's lead role, I was assured, would be played by Jeff Bridges. I was supplied with tapes of Bridges's movies to study and was instructed to write "as if Jeff were in the room with you, cheering you on."

To finance the film, Jean-Paul entertained a steady stream of prospective investors at dinner parties stocked with fashion models and clairvoyants. Part of my job was to attend these parties and "behave like a writer." This involved my talking reassuringly about the progress of the screenplay, only, however, if someone brought up the subject first. Otherwise, I was to be pleasantly drunk, witty if possible, and unobtrusive. I got a sense of how shaky the project was when I saw Jean-Paul frantically put the touch on the wealthy husband of a woman who had been promised a role in the film. It was a fascinating sight, Jean-Paul no taller than five foot four, cornering this guy, threatening to cut the wife out of the action if he didn't come through with the money.

I completed the screenplay, Jean-Paul threw a celebratory dinner, and then word arrived that Jeff Bridges had turned down the part. Jean-Paul went on a two-week bender. His financing had been contingent on Bridges participating in the film. Now he would have to return most of the "development" money he had raised. The money, however, had been spent mounting parties to raise more money. He angrily blamed my screenplay for the setback and dropped out of the project—his way of telling me not to expect to be paid the remainder of what I was owed. Bridges, I later learned, had never laid eyes on my script. His agent would only show it to him if Jean-Paul came up with a letter of credit that proved he could pay Bridges's acting fee in advance.

Now all is forgiven. In retrospect, Jean-Paul's machinations seem harmless and absurd. "I'm producing television commercials these days," he says. He tells me that he has discovered a direct relation between the spiritual emptiness of a product and the viciousness of those who produce it. "For instance, I went to a client's office last week to get paid for an ad campaign. The deal is, I hand over the film and they give me the check. A straight-up exchange. But the client threw my check on the floor. 'Pick it up!' he barked. When I bent over, his assistant rushed me from behind and grabbed the film out of my hand."

As we say goodnight, Jean-Paul asks if I have any new stories to show him. "I'm bored half to death, Michael. Maybe we can get something on."

The Interpreter

FOR A YEAR IN THE LATE 1980S, I worked as an interpreter for Spanish-speaking defendants at Manhattan's criminal court. The job seemed compatible with my writing habit: reasonable hours, lots of spare time, and plenty of interesting human interaction. My inspiration was Daumier and his courthouse sketchbook. I would jot down little vignettes or snippets of conversation overheard between lawyers and their clients. It was a chance to witness the workings of the criminal justice system from backstage.

However, an unexpected feeling of identification with the defendants sabotaged my attempts to maintain an objective eye. We clung to each other with queasy intimacy in the courtroom, as I delivered, in a whisper, the news of their fate, which was almost always bad. In the Tombs, as the jail attached to the courthouse was called, it was worse: prisoners swearing their innocence to their lawyers, vowing revenge, begging me to contact an associate, or experiencing belated seizures of remorse. I lacked the shield of indifference that the job required, a fact that some of the more sharp-eyed felons noted with contempt. "I don't want your pity, *maricon*," a Dominican drug dealer warned me.

It was the height of the crack epidemic and the stream of rapists, child beaters, muggers, and drug fiends seemed endless. After about a month they became like a single person, the composite of failure and despair. My sympathies were mimetic, reflexive, devoid of content. The spell finally broke when I was in court with a repeat violent offender who was about to be sentenced for kidnapping and "deranged indifference." The judge asked him if there was anything he wished to say for the record. The felon launched into a barrage of terrifying threats, each of which he vividly described. I stood mutely by his side until he ran out of steam, at which point I said in my politest voice: "Thank you, your honor. I have nothing to say." Amused, the judge let my omission slide, and handed down the mandatory sentence: twenty-five years with no chance of parole.

Purged of empathy, I joined in the protective cynicism of the courthouse employees. I was an initiate of the system, a member of the guild. Boredom was the permissible emotion. Idealism was regarded as a moral perversion, especially in young public defenders, who were treated with complete disdain. I began to notice the peculiar solicitude with which the officers took custody of a remanded defendant. Prisoners were the meal ticket. "Mutts," they called them. For us, crime was a source of employment. We were the Sisyphean processors of the underclass.

Now, seventeen years later, I have been summoned for jury duty and am back in the courthouse, an immediately familiar world. As soon as I enter the lobby, I remember the suety odor of the Tombs. I pass through the metal detector and ride up to the jury room on the eleventh floor. There is less traffic in the building than in previous years. Crime in Manhattan is on the decline. The elevators are half-empty. In the hallway, I look out the south-facing windows, at the Municipal Building with its wedding-cake tower topped by the sculpture of a golden woman with upraised arms. "Tell her the money's in the freezer," yells a man into his cell phone.

After hanging around for an hour or two, I am marched with a group of prospective jurors to Judge Edwin Torres's courtroom on the ninth floor. A stickup in Washington Heights. One witness. Nobody hurt. A garden-variety crime. I am delighted to see Torres, in his seventies now, with his thin sheath of silver hair and his Nuyorican accent, street-wise and blunt. He was the only Spanish-speaking judge in my day, and the only novelist, having published *Carlito's Way* about an East Harlem thug who becomes a big-time smack trader. Brian De Palma turned it into a movie.

When I am called for *voir dire*, I inform Torres that I used to work in the system. "Did you ever interpret in my court?" I remind him of the case. The year is 1987. An eighty-four-year-old man from Vieques, Puerto Rico. No prior arrests. For eleven consecutive months, after cashing his Social Security check, he was robbed by the same three men. So he bought a handgun on the street for twenty bucks and the next time they tried to mug him he shot one in the chest. The district attorney pressed for manslaughter, but the jury was so charmed by the old man that the DA dropped the charge after the first day at trial. He offered him a plea: possession of an illegal weapon, five years' probation. The old man agreed to the deal.

"They did the right thing," says Torres, remembering the case. Then he asks me the obligatory question: "Do you feel that your experience in the court will prejudice you as a juror?" I describe for him my period of sympathy with the defendants. "I exaggerated their reliance on me. I took on their mannerisms, their tone, though half the time I felt nothing but revulsion."

"I know exactly what you mean," says Torres. "Step down from the jury box. You're excused."

I collect my certificate of service and catch the subway uptown, relieved. The last time I was chosen, I deadlocked a jury for two miserable days. The defendant was a benign-looking man in his fifties, a high school janitor accused of selling dope to students. The only witness was the undercover detective who had busted him. Under cross-examination, the detective admitted that he was racking up as many arrests as possible in order to advance his career. I felt sure that his impatient account of events was a lie. Contributing to this impression was the fact that the city was under pressure to show results in its campaign to clean up the schools.

Among the jurors, however, an elderly woman and I were the only ones who voted for acquittal. We held out for eight hours, and as a result we were all sequestered in a seedy Midtown hotel. The next morning, the woman went over to the other side. "I just want to go home," she explained.

By afternoon, unable to withstand the anger of my fellow jurors, I too voted to convict. Later, I learned that the janitor "took a bullet"—a year in the state penitentiary in Coxsackie—which, his own lawyer assured me, "he richly deserved."

The Bullet

THE NOVELIST WILLIAM HERRICK has died at the age of eighty-nine. Bill, as his friends called him, was the first working writer I had met. I have vivid memories of his study, with its harsh, quarantined air. I would peek into the room when I visited his son, Michael, my boyhood friend. On Bill's desk was a rusted helmet, a piece of shrapnel that he used as a paperweight, and a photograph of his hero, George Orwell. Like Orwell, he had fought against the fascists in the Spanish Civil War—in Herrick's case as a Communist member of the International Brigades. Like Orwell, he had been shot in the neck, the bullet lodging too close to his spine to risk being surgically removed. Like Orwell, he saw the Communists turn their guns on Spanish revolutionaries who did not follow the Stalinist line, an experience that animates at least half of his ten novels. Orwell, however, ended up fleeing the Communists, while fighting with a local militia of independent socialists. Herrick, without meaning to, had been on the side of the hunters.

"There won't be a funeral," says Michael, when phoning with the news. "Ever the realist, Dad donated his body to the Albany Medical Center. 'Just make sure they give us back the bullet,' he said."

"I was suckled on Communism," Bill once told me. "My mother was a charter member of the Party and over my crib hung a piece of tin embossed with the face of Lenin. I could recite the Party line like a catechism, and when the line changed I changed along with it. I was a believer, a fundamentalist. I hated doubt. The party was my faith, my family, my tribe."

Bill was twenty-two in 1936 when he volunteered to fight in Spain, a New York City street kid with little formal education. While convalescing from his gunshot wound at a hospital in Murcia, he wondered aloud about the wisdom of building so many palaces of justice and culture in the Soviet Union. "Don't they need simple places for people to live in?" he asked.

The remark was reported to the Communist chief of security, a German, who took Bill to the basement of a large church on the outskirts of the city where Spanish "Trotskyites" were secretly imprisoned. Herrick was held at gunpoint while three teenagers in rags, one of them a girl, were dragged in front of him, their hands tied with rope. The security chief ordered his henchman, a Belgian, to shoot each one in the back of the skull, after which they were tossed in a corner. "Trotskyite double-dealers," he explained.

The effect on Bill was as if he had pulled the trigger himself, and I sometimes wondered if in fact he had been forced to do so. "I was shaking with shame," he wrote in his memoir, *Jumping the Line*. "These were my comrades, murdering my comrades. . . . And those three Spanish kids. They were me. . . . I had murdered myself."

When he returned to New York, he broke with the Party, not to replace it with another orthodoxy, as some ex-Communists would do, but to hash out, as a writer, his growing disgust with ideology and political power. "My new enemy became my former self," he said. As with Orwell, the moral authority of Herrick's writing is grounded in personal experience. His prose is declarative and raw. "No literary stuff," he used to say with a hint of self-consciousness about his limited schooling. "After all, English is my second language. My first language was the gutter."

In his most powerful novel, *Love and Terror*, Herrick writes about the psychology of terrorism from the inside. Steeling himself for action, the young leader of a Baader-Meinhof–type group repeats his mantra: "The revolution requires that we liquidate our human feeling." He and his comrades hijack a plane and prepare to execute the passengers unless their demands are met. One passenger, an old Communist fighter, recognizes herself in her prospective killers. "These are my children," she thinks, "just as we were Stalin's children. The pretense of certainty. The necessary murder." In the novel, the dictum that "the end justifies the means" becomes, by logical progression, "revolutionary" action for its own sake—a meticulously strategized tantrum with no discernible goal.

I travel to Bill's memorial service at a small Methodist church, which doubles as a synagogue in the town of Old Chatham in upstate New York. Friends and family fondly remember Bill's irascible streak, his appetite, his "scary opinions." His granddaughter recites Kaddish, the prayer for the dead, "though my grandfather was not a religious man," and then, in an almost festive mood we tramp up the road to the family farmhouse where Bill's wife, Jeannette, has laid out a meal.

It is the first mild day of winter, and wooden planks have been placed over the walkway so we don't slip on the melting ice or splash ourselves with mud. The novelist William Kennedy reminisces about the group of writers who used to gather at a saloon in Albany. "Bill was our elder statesman. For years he was the only published novelist among us. He thought I was apolitical. I'm not. But compared to Bill, everyone is."

When the party thins out, Bill's son, Michael, and I drive over to a local bar. I wonder if Bill had been disappointed that Michael had so little interest in politics. "I think he was relieved," says Michael. "He was stuck with the subject, but that didn't mean he wanted his children to be stuck with it too. I imbibed Dad's disillusionment before I had a chance to become disillusioned myself. When as a boy I told him I had joined the Cub Scouts, he said, 'Why do you want to be in a paramilitary organization?' He was right of course."

After a couple of drinks, Michael takes something from his pocket and sets it on the bar. It's the bullet, which the medical center has returned to the family as requested. It's surprisingly slender, no thicker than a pencil, about two inches long, from a Fiat machine gun, Italian made. Encrusted on the brass casing are bits of rough, calcified bone.

I remember a conversation I had with Bill in the 1970s. I had just returned from South America and was telling him about my interest in revolutionary movements. Bill smiled wearily. He reminded me of Chamfort's summation of the French Revolution, which he sometimes quoted in his novels: Be my brother or I will kill you. "I've been hearing those words in one form or another all my life."

I WAS INTRODUCED to the filmmaker Sergio Castilla twenty-five years ago as "an important American author," an absurd exaggeration since all I had published were a couple of juvenile stories and poems. Sergio, more accurately, was presented to me as "a leading Chilean director, in exile after Pinochet's coup d'état." The idea was for us to collaborate on a screenplay, and Sergio showed me his recently completed movie, *Desaparecido*. The film's action takes place in a suburban middle-class house, one of many that were turned into secret torture chambers in Chile during those years. The central character is the commander of the house, a disturbingly charming colonel who treats both his subordinates and victims like misbehaving children. When President Allende's widow saw the movie, she had to excuse herself midway through, explaining to Sergio that she "couldn't bear to see what Chile has come to."

I was familiar with this brand of barbarism, having lived in Argentina during the early days of its Dirty War, and though our writing collaboration didn't work out, Sergio and I became friends. He seemed slightly tortured himself as he raced through New York with a kind of reckless, high-voltage drive. He was furious at Allende for misjudging the fascist insurgency that had gathered force right under his nose. "Idiot humanism," he called it. Since the coup d'état in 1973, he had lived in Stockholm, Havana, Paris, and now Manhattan, starting again from scratch. He wrote his screenplays in quick agitated bursts, one more surreal and bitterly comical than the last. Hollywood was unreceptive, but he made his movies anyway, as if he were mounting a series of guerrilla wars.

After a couple of years he returned to Paris, where, in a film called *Gentille Alouette*, he again satirized the Chilean martinet, through the convoluted relationship of a colonel and his aide.

When we met again, in New York, I was surprised at how much he had changed. He was in psychoanalysis, "looking at everything, *compadre*, peeling myself raw." He announced that if we were to remain friends there was something I needed to know. His father had killed himself before he was old enough to have known him. "He was an East European Jew, a refugee called Moskowitz. I was told he'd had a heart attack and didn't find out the truth until I was eighteen."

He seemed relieved to have disclosed this, as if it were a kind of ultimate cause that explained the course his life had taken. We joked that we were opposites, Sergio diasporic, fatherless, while I was entrenched in New York, saturated in my old man's immigrant ambitions. It fascinated Sergio to hear about my battles with my father, as if I were reminding him of things he too had experienced, but had forgotten. His new movie was a comedy about an eighteen-year-old girl who tries to find the father she never met. She ends up with three claimants to the position, none of them the real one.

With Pinochet out of office he went back to Chile and made two popular movies there, but felt more estranged from his country than ever. "Pinochet is still in power," he told me, "lodged in everyone's psyche, like one of those science-fiction chips that controls your brain. He's the all-powerful father. He threatens you, you obey him, but he punishes you anyway. Until all you want is his approval."

He moved uneasily between Santiago and New York, unwilling to stay put in either city. We wrote another screenplay together, one that attempted to reconcile these two poles. A young American whose father had been a CIA officer in Chile during the 1973 coup becomes romantically involved with a girl whose father is one of the disappeared. They nearly kill each other during a road trip to the far south of Chile, in a primal battle between lovers over history's crimes. We were pleased with the script, but after much agony Sergio backed away from filming it. "I've had it with the coup," he said. "I can't go back to that subject." We argued bitterly over the matter and didn't speak for months.

Now he phones me from the set of his current production, beleaguered but euphoric. "Come over. We'll have lunch. I can use the break."

I visit him on location in Washington Heights, where most of the film's action occurs. "I've never made a movie with so little money," he tells me. "But I don't give a damn." The crew is skeletal, inexperienced, hired on the cheap. Three of the four principal actors have never performed in front of a camera. Two are Dominican, from the neighborhood; all are between eighteen and twenty years old. "My age when I found out about my father," says Sergio. He trained the actors for months, building the script in part out of the raw material of their lives. "I was a brute when I was their age. A drunkard. Stifled. Cut off at the root. I want that feeling from the actors, that sense of primitive desperation."

The street is crowded and hot. A vendor peels a mango with a razor blade, to make it look like a flower. In the near distance are the George Washington Bridge, the bus terminal with its bent metal facade, the stained high-rises that straddle the expressway, and the sprawling hospital, filled with armed guards because Bill Clinton is there, waiting to have his heart repaired.

Sergio leads me into a small private clinic where he and the crew are preparing to shoot a scene. It is supposed to be a psychiatric ward where the main characters meet for the first time. "Would you like to play the psychiatrist?" he asks, handing me a script. I read the part out loud. "You're too seductive, *compadre*. You want everyone to like you."

I give up, unable to play the heavy. But a man arrives whom Sergio spotted earlier on the street in Midtown. Sergio followed the man for three blocks and convinced him to play the role. He is large-bodied and weary, with a vaguely predatory expression. Perfect casting.

23

WITH THE HOPE OF RENTING my apartment while away on vacation, I place an ad on Craigslist. A couple of queries float in that quickly fade away. Then I receive an email from a woman who identifies herself as "Gladys Maestre. MD. PHD. I will be in New York City working as especial faculty at Columbia University," she writes. "How many beds you have?"

I describe my apartment, mentioning my five-year-old son's bedroom. "How many are you?" I ask nervously.

Gladys shoots back with: "We are couple (f + m) with a five-year-old boy that will go to summer camp during the week. Sounds very perfect." She reasonably proposes that her sister-in-law take a look at the apartment. "She is also physician. Also at Columbia. On call tomorrow. She will try to make time for you between patients."

I phone the sister-in-law and arrange for a visit. In the background I hear children squalling. "Are you a pediatrician?" I ask. "*Sí. Pediatra,*" she says after a pause.

A few hours later she arrives at my apartment. She looks about seventeen years old, and is wearing a bright yellow sweatshirt, several sizes too big for her, with an enormous picture of Mickey Mouse. She balances a ten-month-old baby on her hip like a satchel. When it is clear that she does not speak a word of English, I employ the Spanish I learned while living in South America in the 1970s. With that, any pretense of her being a pediatrician is dropped. I hear her mutter "*Mierda!*" as she takes a perfunctory look around the apartment before rushing out the door with her child.

Disaster averted. I never hear from Gladys again. Out of curiosity, I review our correspondence and notice that her Web address is from a server in Colombia. I wonder if Gladys was fronting for a gang of con artists from the School of the Seven Bells in the Colombian highlands, which I have been hearing about for years. Students at Seven Bells learn pick-pocketing, jewelry theft, and various fast-talk cons. For the final exam, a mannequin is dressed in a suit with sleigh bells attached to each of its seven pockets. The student has to lift something from each pocket without ringing a bell.

The incident puts me in mind of my more gullible days, when, in my late teens, I fell under the spell of a self-described grifter named Hugh who hung around the building I lived in on East Ninth Street. I thought of Hugh as an old man, though he was probably no older than forty-five. He was a fastidious junkie in the William Burroughs mold, down to his inexpensive black suits and his interest in unconventional methods of cancer prevention. One such method involved the daily consumption of ozone. Hugh kept a small lead tank of the stuff which he inhaled through a narrow rubber tube.

He was remarkably controlled about his heroin habit. He didn't move in slow motion like other junkies on the street, and I was never certain if he was actually stoned. The key, he told me, was "to know how to stay maintained," which he claimed to do as a member of a pickpocket team, consisting of himself and two partners.

They worked department stores, rock concerts, and the trains that ran along the northeast corridor between Boston and Washington, DC. Hugh liked the trains best because they were lucrative and dangerous; there was nowhere to run if you got nabbed. One partner "fanned the marks," signaling to Hugh where they kept their money. The second partner was cleanup man. Hugh would dish off the wallets to him as soon as he hooked them, thus minimizing the risk of being caught red-handed. After stripping out the cash, the cleanup man would stuff the wallets under seat cushions or push them down the toilet.

Hugh knew I wanted to be a writer, and I realized later that he had been playing that angle, feeding me the kind of material he figured I wished to hear. My weakness, he understood, was a hunger for exotic human attachment, not material greed. He accommodated my romantic view of the low-life and my vanity about being in the know. In return, he was able to learn from me on which day I got paid from the post office where I held a seasonal job. Since I didn't have a bank account, I would immediately turn my paycheck into cash. The cash was what Hugh scored—along with my portable typewriter, my girlfriend's oboe, and her collection of silver bracelets—when he cleaned out our apartment.

I now think of myself as impervious to such cons. However, an encounter the other night with a young man on 108th Street makes me wonder. In gushing, barely coherent Spanish, the man informs me that his three-month-old baby is starving. His wife has no breast milk. As an illegal alien, he does not qualify for public assistance. If he were to apply for it, he would be deported. He has an appointment with the hospital, he says, flashing a stamped, official-looking card, but it isn't until next week. Would I buy him a can of infant formula in the drug store around the corner?

I offer him a couple of bucks, but he refuses the money with an agitated wave of his hand. This is what con artists call "the convincer," and it works. As we enter the drug store, I think of my well-fed son asleep in the apartment. I choose a jumbo can of powdered formula from one of the shelves—twenty-eight bucks for twenty-five ounces. At the checkout counter, the clerk tips me off. "You're the third person I've seen him scam like this today," she says. "The first time he brought the formula back for a refund. The second he probably sold on the street. It's as good as cash."

Before I can confront the grifter, he has darted out the door. I noticed he had a Colombian accent. I wonder if he learned his hustle at the School of the Seven Bells.

It is the first time I have fallen for a street con since Hugh, thirty years ago, and I am oddly relieved to discover that I still have the capacity to be fooled. I remember the origin of the term *confidence man*. A well-dressed individual approached a stranger on the street. "Do you have enough confidence in humankind to let me hold your watch?" he asked. When handed the watch, the man walked away with it.

If You Expect Gratitude, You're Doomed

24

AFTER LISTENING TO ME go on about the lousy food in our neighborhood restaurants, a friend suggested that I visit the soup kitchen at the Broadway Presbyterian Church on 114th Street. "The chef there, Michael Ennes, is a master," my friend said. "He's cooked in some of the city's top kitchens, and on a good day his lunch is equal to any on the Upper West Side." For a couple of months last year my friend worked for Chef Michael as a volunteer. "He hustles up prime leftovers from his contacts in the trade." One day, twenty pounds of morel mushrooms showed up from Le Bernardin on 51st Street. They had been slightly overcooked. "Morels cost two hundred bucks a pound when dry. Michael used them for soup stock."

Out of curiosity, I walked over to the church, and made my way down to the basement where the stiffening whiff of disinfectant was improbably overpowered by the smell of nutmeg emanating from Chef Michael's domain. He is a large, bearded, big-voiced man in his mid-fifties, with a face reddened from splash burns suffered at the stove. His chef's hat was a French Revolutionary's cockade, and his black smock had his name embroidered in red thread over the chest pocket.

"Either we hang together or hang alone," he said by way of greeting, quoting one of his heroes, Tom Paine. He paddled a vat of black bean soup, then scooped portions of cheese fondue onto tortilla chips. "A little appetizer." The fondue came from the morning television *Today Show*. As a stunt to get into the Guinness Book of Records, the show had prepared 225 gallons of the stuff in front of the camera. "Fortunately, it freezes well," said Michael.

In the dining room, about 140 homeless people were sitting at a dozen round tables, like attendees at an awards banquet, patiently waiting to be served. Customers aren't obliged to stand in line, as in other soup kitchens, because it's humiliating, according to Michael. "They become pushy and anxious and hard." No one is turned away, no matter the shape he or she is in, and a few of the diners appeared to be in extreme states of distress. They cover a wide range, however: at one of the tables I spotted a young woman with a long braided pigtail, designer glasses, and a large turquoise ring, scrolling intently through her cellphone.

I ventured a glance at the sign-up sheet that everyone is required to fill out, though no proof of identity is demanded. Among the diners on the list were Barack Obama, George W. Bush, Michael Jordan, and Tiger Woods. Seeing me scanning the sheet, a volunteer grabbed it away. "This is confidential information," he said.

Realizing I was standing in the middle of the room and that people were eyeing me suspiciously from their seats, I sat down awkwardly in one of the few vacant chairs. The man next to me gripped his newspaper so I wouldn't steal it. Then, a heavy-set man with an enormous Afro accused me of being an FBI agent. He rushed toward me. "I know who you are," he said, and punched me sharply in the ribs. A sigh seemed to go around the room, or perhaps a twitter of laughter. I assured him that we had never met, dropping my eyes because the stare in which we were locked seemed to agitate him further. My neighbor with the newspaper explained: "It's because you're carrying that pad. Folks don't like it when you write things down."

I retreated to the kitchen where, with some effort, Michael was carrying out the black bean soup. "Hot stuff coming through!" Next came fresh vegetables with rice, and a salad of organic lettuce that looked superior to the greens I routinely overpaid for at the specialty market near my apartment.

The main course consisted of catfish fillets in a remoulade sauce. Cooling on a rack was the peach crumble Michael had baked for dessert. He worried if there would be enough. "Did anyone complain that the catfish was too spicy?" He endeavored both to please his customers and to protect them from themselves. Pouring sugar into a huge vat of tea, he said: "They'll grumble that it's too bitter. But you can't put sugar on the table with this crowd. They'll ignore the scoop spoon and tip the entire bowl over into their teacups. It's not their fault, of course. Alcohol and heroin addiction have dulled their sugar receptors."

When I stopped by the kitchen again a few days later, Michael was in a sour mood. In a pinch he had been forced to make do with hot dogs for his main course. "Industrial food of the worst kind. And a complete bore to prepare." It reminded him of when he first started cooking at the church six years ago. "We were just another dump site for surplus goods from the government food bank: canned corn and processed cheese, most of which was about to expire." This had been shortly after the attacks on the World Trade Center, when New York's restaurants were strapped and Michael was between jobs. "I was constitutionally unable to serve that junk, so I found the food I wanted."

A well-dressed woman in her sixties who had been volunteering as a server came into the kitchen, visibly distraught. "I'm leaving now, Michael, and I won't be back." One of the customers had insulted her, saying she was too slow to bring him his food, and ridiculing her gray hair. "My feelings of charity have reached their limit," she said. I asked if it was the man with the Afro. "God, no. He's a perfect gentleman."

Michael thanked her and wished her luck. "If you expect gratitude around here, you're doomed," he said to me after she had gone. He guessed the culprit was one of the new middle-class clients. "The fastest-growing group we have." Most had lost their apartments, scorched by the real-estate boom. "They're difficult to help because they have no street smarts, and they're pissed off and demanding."

One man used to arrive at the soup kitchen in his Jaguar, his last valuable possession and the one he refused to part with. He claimed to have worked for the FBI, and during the height of the terrorist frenzy talked himself into a job as a security analyst for CNN. "He lasted there for three weeks." Fancying himself a restaurant critic, he would occasionally send back his plate with a note informing Michael of his displeasure. "He ended up selling books from the sidewalk on Broadway."

25

WHO HASN'T ENCOUNTERED MADNESS at some point in their lives, in a relative or a friend? About 2.5 percent of the population has schizophrenia or manic-depressive psychosis, a fraction that is the same in every corner of the world regardless of cultural distinctions. As a boy I used to listen with fascination while my manic uncle had it out with his phantoms. Another family member is similarly afflicted. And my daughter suffered a stabbing breakdown in 1996, when she was fifteen. Psychiatrists tell me it's a case of genetic bad luck, but one can't be sure. The fundamental mechanisms of psychosis are as mysterious as they have ever been.

There may no more be a solution to insanity than there is a key to consciousness itself, and our attempts to find one—from the priestly attentiveness of Freud to the chemical tinkering of pharmacologists with the brain's limbic system, the way the Federal Reserve tinkers with the money supply to keep the economy from crashing—merely reflect our wish to tame an unknowable area of existence.

What has set me thinking about this are the inconspicuous iron teeth that have been fastened to the top of the stone surround of my building on Manhattan's Upper West Side. They have been put there to keep the mentally ill at the treatment center across the street from lounging in front of our sunny, south-facing door. I wince when I witness how effective the teeth are. A small, hunched-over woman, to whom I often nod good morning, innocently sits down, is jabbed by the iron, jumps to her feet, tries sitting again, then shuffles away, bewildered.

"Is this necessary?" I ask the building superintendent who installed the device.

"Talk to your neighbors," he says. "It was their idea."

As it happens, our tenants' association is scheduled to meet in a few days. I decide to attend and present a case for having the iron teeth removed.

One is wary of being like those who bleed for the helpless while nursing an attitude of suspicion toward the rest of humankind, but what exactly is my neighbors' complaint against these people? They don't spread litter. Doughnuts and tobacco are their only apparent vices. They're gone before dark, carried away in chauffeured vans to group homes in other parts of the city. As for noise: there are only brief bursts of hilarity, followed by extended bouts of medicated silence. I begin to see those little teeth as a kind of Cerberus guarding against a terrifying, and seemingly arbitrary, misfortune. Do Not Curse Our Door.

To build my case for the tenants' meeting, I visit the treatment center where, with enthusiasm, I am invited to make myself at home. I've been to places like this in the past and am familiar with their pleasant laid-back feeling, like stepping into a low-pressure cocoon. Idleness is tolerated. Smoking is embraced as an essential facet of existence. Most impulses toward self-expression appear to be encouraged, if not indulged.

A woman whom I recognize as one of the regulars on the street approaches me as I admire an art exhibit on the wall. "That's mine," she says, pointing to a violent, carefully rendered drawing of armed warriors entitled "The Assault." Worried that I might be disturbed by her creation, she whispers, "Don't take it too literally; it only comes from my mind."

On the bulletin board is a notice for a writing workshop in the afternoon. Participants will be published in an anthology titled "Outsider Poems "that is put out by the center. For the purpose of job training, a comfortable alcove has been turned into the replica of a restaurant coatroom. People are exchanging torn umbrellas and jackets for numbered cards, which they later bring back to be redeemed. "One of our clients just landed work checking coats at the Plaza Hotel," a member of the staff informs me. This is exactly the kind of job I used to look for when I was younger (late-night hotel clerk was another). The idea was to find work in which I could observe people, write, and get paid at the same time.

Other parallels between myself and the center's "clients" occur to me, not least of which is our dubious value to the gross national product. Such comparisons, however, only go so far. With her picked skin and fallen stockings, the woman who created "The Assault" reminds me of the business at hand.

With a welcoming handshake, the director of the center invites me into his office. His inspiration, he tells me, is the "moral treatment" devised by the French reformer Philip Pinel in the 1820s. "The point is simply for my clients to be here," the director says. "Showing up is an end in itself. It facilitates personal attachment. We believe people change for the sake of maintaining relationships. It's an old-fashioned idea. But it works the way nothing else has in five hundred years of failed therapies."

When he learns I live across the street, his manner abruptly changes. He is accustomed to his clients being treated as pariahs and assumes that I've come with a list of complaints. I try to explain that my aim is to have those vicious teeth in front of my building removed. This doesn't seem to register, however. He retreats into an impenetrable public-relations zone.

The following morning, I think about what I might say at the tenants' meeting. I've never been to one of these gatherings and I am nervous, unsure. I'll open with a glowing description of the center. Our neighborhood used to be known as Bloomingdale, I might point out, after the Bloomingdale Lunatic Asylum, famous in its day for its enlightened treatment of the insane. This should have a positive impact on my neighbors: the mad, like the Indians, were here before we were. I rehearse Foucault's argument that the presence of madness on our doorstep is good for us, for it reminds us that the life we live is merely one among several human possibilities. Plato believed that insanity was essential to our nature and assumed that it held esoteric knowledge about who we are. We shouldn't be chasing these people away, we should be welcoming them, thanking them for forcing us into this debate with ourselves . . .

I try out these thoughts on a couple who live on the floor below. When I finish, there's an annoyed silence. "Not everyone has your superior moral fiber," says the husband.

Later, I run into the center's director at the coffee shop on the corner. "You'll be pleased to hear this," he says brightly. "We're building a roof deck for our clients. They won't be harassing you any longer."

The tenants' meeting is scheduled for eight o'clock that evening. I decide to stay home.

26

IN JULY 1991, while digging the foundation for a skyscraper at Broadway and Reade Street in lower Manhattan, excavators stumbled upon a portion of the "Negros Burial Ground," the only prerevolutionary African cemetery known to exist in the United States. A map of Manhattan from 1755 had provided the principal evidence of the burial ground's existence. It had covered six acres, roughly five present-day city blocks, from 1650 until 1794, when it was claimed by real-estate expansion and built over without so much as a marker. In 1865, a historian described the cemetery as "an unattractive and desolate" place where "by permission the slave population were allowed to inter their dead."

Excavation for the skyscraper was immediately halted. The *New York Times* declared it "one of the nation's most important archaeological finds of this century." A team of diggers brought up more than four hundred skeletons, some with coins in their hands and over their eyes. "Almost all were buried in coffins," said Ed Rutsch, leader of the dig. "We had expected to find them only in shrouds."

After a couple of months, archaeologists were estimating that the African Burial Ground, as it is now called, contained as many as twenty thousand graves, a far greater number than had been believed. It dispelled the illusion of many New Yorkers that, owing to its numerous abolitionist associations and large population of black fugitives from the South, the city had been only peripherally involved in the slave trade.

One afternoon in August, my friend Roy and I wandered over to Reade Street and watched the diggers fussily sift through the earth with their trowels. "Isn't whitey something," cracked Roy in his slightly bitter manner. "Exhuming old slave bones. Exactly what you don't want us Negroes to be thinking about."

By "you" Roy meant white liberal New Yorkers, of which, according to him, I was a prime example. Our friendship was predicated on a punishing frankness, and for years we had bantered about slavery and color-hate in a series of purgative exchanges that often left us depleted and disturbed.

August 1991 was also the month that riots erupted between Orthodox Jews and blacks in Crown Heights, Brooklyn. Roy and I mimicked the battle. A whole new set of antagonisms seemed to surge to the surface. "All during my growing-up years, you were the landlord, the grocer, demanding money, the only whitey we ever dealt with near home. The pathetic white sharecropper with his stupid slave."

I replied that at least Jews brought business to the neighborhood. Who else would have bothered to risk it? "All we ever got for our trouble was a kick in the teeth. Do you think we don't know what it's like to be despised?" I asked. To which Roy answered, "The pity is, you can see yourself in the nigger, but not how the nigger sees you."

I wondered if we weren't caught in some elaborate psychic trap, like the black man and the Jew in Bernard Malamud's novel *The Tenants*. The only ones left in a condemned Manhattan building, they compete for the same (white) woman, embrace like long lost brothers, and eventually rip each other to shreds.

Born in 1939, Roy grew up before the civil-rights era in an all-black pocket of Jamaica, Queens. His father was dark-skinned and his mother was a "red-bone," part Cherokee with lofty cheeks, "the closest my old man could get to the white women he spent his life gazing at with murder and lust." For Roy, slavery's most evil aftereffect was his own fixation on white women, which appeared to rule his existence. He had a never-ending procession of white girlfriends. It always seemed to end badly, with humiliation and numbness on Roy's part. Black women, on the other hand, were on a higher plane, pure in some intrinsic way, and beyond desire.

Shortly after we met, Roy gave me Richard Wright's story "The Man Who Killed a Shadow" to read. In the story, a "tiny, blonde, blue-eyed . . . crackpot" hikes her dress around her thighs and orders the black janitor, who is the story's protagonist, to clean under her desk. The janitor demurs. She calls him a "black nigger." Overtaken by a sense "of wild danger," he slaps her. She screams "as if he has raped her," and he finds himself "in the worst trouble that a black man could imagine." To stop her screaming, he picks up a split log from a nearby fireplace and kills her.

"You see how it is," said Roy when I returned the book to him. "A miserable, incurable disease."

Two years after the riots in Crown Heights and the unearthing of the African Burial Ground, Roy was diagnosed with advanced prostate cancer. To prolong his life he would have to cease producing testosterone and submit to what his doctor called "medical castration." Despite my attempts to convince him not to, Roy refused treatment. "Should it surprise you, Michael, that my sex drive is lethal," he said, closing the subject for good.

Recently, I visited the exhibition Slavery in New York at the New-York Historical Society on Central Park West. On display are pictures of the skeletons that were dug up at Reade Street. The magnitude of the cemetery has prompted historians to revise their view of the importance of slavery in colonial New York. For portions of the seventeenth and eighteenth centuries, it turns out, New York housed the largest urban slave population on the continent. The city's slave market was at the foot of Wall Street where, in 1752, an African cost Pounds 27, the present-day equivalent of about six thousand dollars.* Rebellion was a constant fear. No more than twelve slaves were permitted to attend a funeral, which, to suppress the African custom of burying by night "with mummeries and outcries," could take place only during daytime. New York did not abolish slavery until 1827, fifty years after Vermont and forty-four after Massachusetts.

In December 1993, shortly before he died, Roy and I were in a bar when a news flash on the television reported that a black man had opened fire on a New York commuter train

*Calculated in dollars as of 2005.

during rush hour, killing five whites and wounding twenty others. "If you knew how many black people walk around fantasizing about doing just what that guy did, you'd never leave your apartment," Roy said. He thoroughly approved when, in court, acting as his own lawyer, the murderer pleaded innocent on the grounds that racism had driven him insane.

Hart Island

I FIRST BECAME AWARE of Hart Island while flying into LaGuardia Airport on a clear morning several years ago. It seems a curious place from the air, 101 acres of half-wild land in the shape of a T-bone steak off the far eastern coast of the Bronx on Long Island Sound. Peering down, I could make out a flat, treeless landscape, with a few derelict buildings, a ferry slip, and a couple of trenches with a handful of men standing around them, apparently working.

Later, I learned that what I had been looking at was New York City's potter's field, the most populous cemetery in America, with 800,000 bodies buried in unmarked mass graves. The workers were inmates from Rikers Island. They had been standing in a burial pit, stacking the pine caskets that the city supplies for its unclaimed dead. They place the caskets along a tight grid, like laying brick, three deep and 150 per grave for adults, five deep and 1,000 per grave for babies, who comprise about half the dead in potter's field. It might take months or even a year to fill a grave, after which it blends quickly into the landscape, invisible except for a single concrete block with a number on it to mark the location, in the event that any of the bodies need to be disinterred.

Not long ago I attempted to visit Hart Island, but was barred from riding the ferry. It's operated by the Department of Corrections, and carries only trucks from the city's various morgues, the inmate laborers, and their guards. "It would be a security risk, both for you and the mutts," explained an officer, referring to the inmates.

No one lived on the island: the prisoners arrived in the morning and left to go back to their cells in the afternoon. Burial detail was Tuesday through Friday. Mondays were reserved for disinterment, a service for family members who had been unable to claim their dead during the two weeks the morgue was required to keep them, and now wanted to bury them elsewhere. Weekends, the island was deserted, with no conceivable risk to visitors or anyone else. It was the city's public cemetery, I argued, I just wanted to have a walk around. "We don't encourage curiosity seekers," I was told. To go there, I would have to prove that I had a relative buried on the island, and though I probably had several from my family's first years in New York, tracing one of them would have involved entering a costly bureaucratic labyrinth that was beyond me.

Last week, a friend introduced me to the artist Melinda Hunt, who has been boring through the bureaucratic and metaphysical mysteries of Hart Island since 1991. "The quintessential place of eternal urban anonymity," Melinda calls it.

She is a thin, serious, attentive woman who grew up in Alberta, Canada, and came to New York in 1988 when she was twenty-nine. Her feeling for the city seems urgent and intense. She told me that after becoming a U.S. citizen, her impulse was to "dive down and explore the depths of my new culture. I'm an immigrant. And potter's field is where immigrants are buried."

In March 1992, Melinda got permission to travel to Hart Island and ask the inmates on burial detail to write down their thoughts. "The truck bringing the bodies was late and we were standing in the cold around this huge empty trench, waiting," she said. "A perfect opportunity for reflection." Melinda received a grant to hang the testimonials as part of a sculpture installation in City Hall Park, which had been the site, in the seventeenth century, of both the British Commons and New York's first potter's field. "The almshouse had been there, the British barracks, the jail, the workhouse, the hospital, and the burial ground—the same institutions that are linked to Hart Island today. I wanted people to think about that, to make the connection between then and now."

As it happened, it also abutted the site of the old Negros Burial Ground. The exact boundaries between the two cemeteries were uncertain. "American prisoners were buried there during the Revolutionary War," said Melinda. "Revolutionary artifacts were found in those graves. History points to the Negros Burial Ground being a mixed place. Anyone who was outside the reigning social structure was buried there: slaves, non-Christians, paupers, the mad."

After learning of Melinda's proposed installation, Howard Dobson, head of the Schomburg Center for Research in Black

Culture, accused her of "doing white man's history." According to Dobson, she was trying to rob African Americans of a sacred piece of their history.

With that, her project was canceled, and her funding withdrawn. "I became an instant pariah. I was cut off. No one would return my phone calls." All of the testimonials she had gathered were written by black inmates. "An American friend tried to explain it to me: 'Black people don't want white people talking about black people in prison.' I think he was right. As a Canadian, I didn't understand racial politics in America."

DNA analysis of the bones would have settled the controversy, but after a protest the bones were removed from a "white" forensic lab and sent to an archaeologist at Howard University, who pronounced them African bones, slave bones, without testing the DNA. Eventually, Melinda won a lawsuit against the city for violation of her first amendment rights, but by then it was too late: her exhibition permit had long since expired.

The experience seemed to intensify her connection to Hart Island, as if she too had been buried in a figurative potter's field. More than a place to live, New York had become an occupation to her, its callousness and social complexities a source of bewilderment and creative drive.

Last year, under the Freedom of Information Law, she obtained a record of everyone who has been buried on Hart Island since 1985—1,300 pages with 49,400 names. "I'm handing them out. Anyone who emails me with a confirmed date of death post-1985 gets a page."

As we were talking, she received a request from a woman looking for her uncle who died on February 26, 1989. Within minutes, Melinda found his grave number.

"I tried to take Hart Island to City Hall Park, the former Commons," she said with satisfaction. "Now I'm building a new Commons, a metaphorical Commons, around the burial records."

As I was leaving, she handed me one of the inmate testimonials she had wanted to hang in City Hall Park. It was written in charcoal in a careful hand. "My name is Eddie Melendez. When I first came to heart island It was just a job to me. But when I found out that my baby sister was beried hear It hurt me. Because. She didn't get a proper berial. For I can pay my restpeck's and now I beiry a baby I think of my sister. I feal that they should put a memorial plack for all the children's and peaple that are beiryed hear. For the peaple in the city can see all the peaple that are beired hear."

28

I'VE BEEN HANGING AROUND Central Park for more than forty years, and even slept there for two nights after brawling with my father at the age of fourteen, bathing in the model-boat pond at 74th Street and getting mugged by teenagers wielding wooden planks with bent nails in them in the North Woods. But walking in the park last week with the writer and naturalist Marie Winn, I felt as if I had stepped into a fantastical world to which I was a complete stranger.

We entered at the Explorers' Gate on West 77th Street about an hour before sunset, Marie with a bag on each shoulder and a pair of binoculars round her neck, hobbling slightly on a sore foot that she refuses to allow to curtail her daily expeditions. "I heard an unusual insect the other night and followed it to a mulberry tree. But I couldn't find it. It's early for crickets. The sound has been haunting me all week." With the intense feeling for Manhattan's wildlife that has caused her innumerable bouts of euphoria and heartache, she wondered if it could have been some sort of cry. "Central Park is perfectly self-enclosed, sometimes tragically so," she said, "which is precisely the source of its drama and magic." A third of the eight hundred bird species in North America pass through Central Park every year, making it a major site for birding, equal to the Florida Everglades and Yosemite.

We headed north to Turtle Pond, its surface covered in a lime-green carpet of duckweed, where Marie directed my attention to a black-crowned night heron violently shaking a smallmouth bass in his beak before swallowing it in a rippling gulp. She appreciated my thrilled astonishment, but didn't seem to share it. She was familiar with that bird, and recalled the time it had tried to make a meal out of a family of baby green herons that were nesting nearby. "The babies' parents barely managed to thwart him. It was an anxious period for us all."

She led me to a thriving linden tree on the edge of the Great Lawn. "The Robin Boys Dormitory," Marie called it, sitting me down on a bench to behold the spectacle of hundreds of robins streaming on to its branches, "like a plume of smoke," jostling for good spots to roost in a piercing pre-bedtime racket. She pointed out their red breasts: every one of them was male, sent away by nesting females to sleep on their own until September. "Don't they sound like boys?"

At nine o'clock the robins suddenly fell silent, as if they had fallen asleep at the same time. A dozen raccoons invaded our bench, portly and brazen, crowding around Marie who removed a cookie from one of her bags and broke off little chunks for them. "The mouse in my office turns its nose up at cookies. It prefers rice cakes." The raccoons seemed unappeased, and Marie explained that they were looking for a

Russian woman in a wheelchair who regularly brought them a vat of macaroni and cheese.

Our final stop was the model-boat pond, where a black skimmer flew noiselessly along the surface of the water, its orange-and-black bill making a razorlike wake behind it. Marie seemed as mesmerized as I was, though she had seen it a hundred times, tilting her body when the skimmer reached the end of the pond to make its wide, elegant turn. "Their presence in the park is a mystery," she said. "No one knows where they come from or where they go when they leave." She closed her eyes. "If you listen closely you can hear its beak snap." Evidently, some New Yorkers empty their fish tanks into the pond before leaving town on vacation, providing the skimmer with an inexhaustible supply of food.

The next day, still under the spell of our excursion, I emailed Marie to thank her, and she invited me to go owling. "Meet me at the 103rd Street gate. 7.30." I understood this was an honor. In her book, *Central Park in the Dark*, Marie writes about the strict rules of owl etiquette: "The exact location of a roosting owl is never revealed," lest someone should decide to scoop it, sleeping, from its perch and make a doomed pet of it.

I followed her down a narrow welted path, along a stream called the Loch, into the marshy North Woods, the wildest area of the park, and not far from the spot where I was mugged forty years ago. Three owlers had arrived before us, regular members of Marie's band. I gathered from their friendly greeting that she had told them about me beforehand. One had a Nikon camera with a paparazzo-strength 500-millimeter lens, aimed at a stand of thin trees where a family of screech owls were known to roost.

At sunset, one began to stir, limbering up and preening. Then it flew out with a quick downward dive. When it was mobbed by a group of anxious catbirds, one of the owlers spotted it on a log by the Loch. I was electrified and could sense the rapture of the others. The owl was seven feet from us, its eyes glowing, while members of its family called out from the roost tree to let it know they were near, each with its distinctive whinny or trill. "The babies are finding their singing style," whispered the man with the camera. Then it was dark, and we lost track of them.

I knew from Marie that their survival was a kind of miracle. Screech owls had been common in Central Park until the 1950s, when they were wiped out by cars, to which they are particularly vulnerable because of their plunging flight that levels off at two or three feet from the ground. Eight or nine years ago, in an attempt to reintroduce them to the park, thirty-two screech owls were let loose, each equipped with a tiny radio transmitter "in a mini-backpack attached to the bird by Teflon ribbons." It took about a month for the owls to ditch the backpacks, and the park rangers seemed to lose interest in them. By the beginning of last winter none had been spotted for a long while and the population was presumed to have perished, killed by cars, each other, or preyed upon by a great horned owl, an escaped pet as it turned out, who unexpectedly dallied in the park for almost an entire winter. With a boom box Marie had "broadcast the screech owl's songs, from the North Woods to Central Park South . . . and no bird sang back."

In February, however, she and her cohorts discovered this family. The babies hatched in April. Marie remembers them when their beaks were still bare. "Our addiction stays alive," she said, as we made the five-minute hike back into the city.

Dachshund

29

ON MONDAY I get a call from a friend who lives upstate. About a year ago he took in our dog, Eli, whom we had exiled due to his tendency to bite children. Our son was one of his victims, as were two of his playmates. "He's the first dog that I've failed to find good rapport with," says my friend. "I never imagined it possible. I tried to encourage him to develop his own interests, but he has no sense of autonomy. He's a bottomless pit of need." That evening he drives down to Manhattan in his pickup truck, drops Eli at our apartment, and heads back to the country.

Eli is a miniature wire-haired dachshund. Shortly after he was born, his breeder gave him to us free of charge, explaining that he had "a disgraceful domed head," a propensity to be overweight, and was sure to develop back trouble in middle age. Moreover, she said, he was "pessimistic and whiny." I liked this description. It made him sound like a cross between Truman Capote and Norman Mailer.

As a puppy, Eli lived up to this billing: he was imaginative, easily threatened, and buffoonishly vicious. With his domed head in my lap, my warm feelings toward him are immediately rekindled. Maybe we can keep him, I think. Our son is four now, old enough to learn how to deal with his eccentricities.

Tuesday. Time to take Eli out for his walk. En route to the lobby, the elevator stops on the second floor. In staggers a toddler, followed by her mother. The toddler lunges excitedly at Eli, grabbing a fistful of his short, wiry hair. Eli hunches into a frozen ball. A dull look comes into his eyes and the corners of his lips curl upward. I scoop him off the floor, knocking the toddler out of the way in the process. She clutches her mother's leg, bawling. "I was worried he might snap at her," I explain. "Then he shouldn't be around children!" the mother shouts. I think of the passage in Revelation about "dogs, sorcerers, whoremongers, murderers, and idolaters" being barred from the City of God.

Wednesday. Without hiding his faults, we advertise Eli's availability on a dachshund Web site. A woman called Aubrey responds. She invites Eli to her duplex in Greenwich Village where she lives with two cats and a well-groomed dachshund. The dachshund lounges glamorously in a velveteen bed on the floor. The apartment is spotless. There are no children in the building. "Poor Harry is lonely," says Aubrey of her dachshund. "He wants a friend." The dogs ignore each other, which Aubrey claims is proof of Harry's "unconditional acceptance" of Eli. "What's his astrological sign?" she asks. He was born in early January. "Hmm. A Capricorn." Aubrey was born under the sign of Aries. "We're not a perfect match, but it doesn't have to be a disaster." When she learns I'm a Scorpio, she moves a few inches away on the couch.

Harry, as it happens, has problems of his own. He's a "submissive urinator" who pees in the apartment. Eli, I proudly inform her, is well trained in this respect. He may be able to help Harry get over his hang-up. Aubrey is more interested in plumbing the depths of Eli's character, which I hear myself describing with unexpected emotion. He wants something only after others have shown they want it first, I tell her. A ball, for instance. Or affection. Even food. Once his desire is aroused he becomes fixated. He pesters you to console him, but when you do, it seems to increase his misery. What I value about Eli, I realize, is that he makes me feel less neurotic. "Let me think it over for a few days," Aubrey says.

Saturday. Aubrey suggests we join her at Washington Square Park where the Dachshund Friendship Club is holding its annual festival. With Eli by my side I am embraced at once by the crowd, which is huddled in a light drizzle under the arch. A man whose "twin minis" are tricked out in identical top hats and skirts, presses me to contribute to his dachshund rescue fund. Sheet music is passed round as an accordion player and a fiddler launch into a beerhall polka called "The Dachs Song": "There's no other dog like a dachshund,/ Walking so close to the ground/They're stubborn and sly as a fox and/The happiest pet to be found." I glance at the rescue fund man, singing with gusto, his twins looking anxious and trapped. Aubrey agrees to take Eli back to her duplex for a sleepover, on trial.

Sunday. The Feast of St. Francis, patron saint of animals. The Cathedral of St. John, near my apartment on the Upper

West Side, is mobbed. Thousands stand in line with their pets, waiting to be blessed by the dean and his ministers. A camel arrives in a trailer, then an elephant, an eagle, a horse. They are escorted up the stone steps like dignitaries, their attendants dressed in sandals and long Franciscan robes. Animal breath fills the cathedral, which is swarming with house pets of every conceivable ilk—ferrets, skunks, bees, chickens, tortoises, lizards, and the peacocks who live on the cathedral grounds. "Look at the wild beasts of the earth," says the dean. "They do not worry about tomorrow. Tomorrow will bring worries of its own." Worshipers kneel with their arms around their pets, as the incense bearers swing their censers, barefoot children wave colored flags, and three handlers try to yank a reluctant boar down the center aisle. Its long snout and suffering air remind me of Eli.

The lead story in the tabloids that day is in perfect tune with the spirit of St. Francis: "A 400-pound tiger that mauled its animal-loving owner was lugged out of a Harlem apartment after a commando-style operation by police," writes a reporter in the *Daily News*. Tiger Man, as some New Yorkers are calling the owner, skipped town with his wounds and was arrested in Philadelphia. He had acquired the tiger as a kitten, adding it to a menagerie that included, at various times, an alligator, monkeys, and a hyena. The tiger had its own bedroom with a built-in sandbox. Tiger Man would feed it by throwing in bags of raw chicken and slamming the door. Eventually he let the animals have the apartment for themselves, which in Manhattan is the ultimate sacrifice. Most of his neighbors didn't mind. "He took care of his pets," said one. "To me, that's cool."

Feeling slightly forlorn in our creatureless apartment, I phone Aubrey to find out how Eli is getting on. "He slept in my bed last night. Even Harry is warming to him. I really like his intensity. I think I'm going to keep him."

Monday. Tiger Man appears in court, his mauled arm in a sling. After being charged with reckless endangerment and possession of a wild animal, he says, "I want my cat back. He was like a child with a loaded gun. Unpredictable. Sad. I loved him anyway."

30

OUR NEIGHBOR MICHEL on Cape Breton Island, where we are taking a summer break from New York, invites my wife, our son Brendan, and me over for dinner. Leg of goat is served from a former member of Michel's herd. During the meal, one of the guests remembers holding the goat down while Michel castrated it. "I had to put plugs in my ears, the shrieking was so loud." The women chime in with a few inquiries about technique. At the mention of "testicles" the children fall to the floor laughing.

Carving the meat, however, Michel is serious and sad. He remembers "executing" the goat with Patrice from across the road, who butchered it in return for a shoulder. Although it is far from the first animal Michel has killed, the memory distresses him. "An attachment is formed. I ask myself, 'Who am I to be playing God?'"

One of his goats peers in the window at us with its glistening walnut hair. In the yard, the chickens run away from the dogs with brief, panicked cries. I ask for a second helping. If anything, the talk lends an aura to the meat, an authenticity. "Michael, you need to kill what you eat, for once," says Michel. "It'll make you more honest."

It is true that I have never killed my food, other than a fish here and there, but is this something to be corrected? I remember an incident in Mendoza, Argentina, in 1972. For a story I was writing, I assisted a family of sharecroppers with the harvesting of their wine grapes. When the grapes were in, I was presented with a live chicken for a celebratory meal. "Wring its neck," I was told. I tried, half-heartedly, and the bird wrestled free of my grasp, raising a flutter of dust as it hit the ground. Everyone laughed. This was exactly what they had expected of me. *Sabe comer pero no puede matar,* remarked the head of the family. He can eat but he cannot kill. His elderly mother scooped up the bird, quickly snapped its neck, and dropped it into the raised hammock of her dress for plucking.

The next morning I phone Michel to thank him for dinner, and end up telling him about the chicken in Mendoza. "You need to finish the job," he says. "I'm going to find you something to kill. I promise." Don't go out of your way, I want to answer. But he has already hung up.

A few days later, I run into him on our dirt road. With a hint of resentment he lets me know that his efforts on my behalf have turned into an ordeal. He had planned to give me one of his own birds to kill, "but the time isn't right, she's still laying." One friend offered him a hen. "It felt like an old lady, all frail in my arms. It would be inedible. I couldn't accept it." Finally, he traded two pounds of the feta cheese he makes from his goat milk for a "meat bird."

"I didn't like being the one to choose it," he says. "That should have been your job. Playing God."

I go to his house to meet "my" bird. It looks anxious and soiled in a wire cage. Michel's chickens run free in the yard. "I tell myself they have a happy life," he says. "But how would I know? Maybe it's only their misery that I would recognize."

As I sharpen his ax, he tells me of his arrival in Cape Breton, from Montreal, sixteen years ago, completely alone. "I came here on a whim. I had no idea how to live in such a place. I just wanted to be thrown on myself, without distractions." Since childhood, he has had a powerful feeling for animals. Now he slaughters them occasionally, though only, he points out, for his family's food.

He takes the ax from my hand. "That's good enough. It's never been sharper." And I realize that he is setting me up in order to try to catch a glimpse of himself, at his own first killing, from the outside.

Our plan is to eat the chicken on Saturday, and with the idea of practicing my stroke, I take the ax home with me. I draw a mark on a tree stump similar to the one on which I am to perform the act. I hit the mark easily a couple of times, then, worried that the blade might become dull, I stow the ax under the porch.

On Saturday, I remove it and walk down the hill to Michel's. The chicken seems more comfortable in its cage. "I believe they're born with some kind of merciful foreknowledge of their fate," he says. "None of these meat birds lasts more than ten weeks."

I reach into the cage and grab its legs, slightly sticky and smooth like the underbelly of a snake. I hold it upside down so that the blood flows to its head, as Michel advised me to do. The chicken goes limp. I arrange it on the tree stump, where it lies as patiently as Isaac. The neck looks small, obscured by feathers, a difficult target, I think. The ax feels too large, more suited to the felling of young trees than fowl. "What are you waiting for!" shouts Michel.

I let the blade fall, more like a tap than a chop, as if I am trying to get the bird's attention. It immediately awakens from its trance, squawking wildly. I haven't kept my end of the bargain. I strike again, harder. A third chop does the job. Delicately, as if not to harm it, I place it in the plastic bucket Michel has supplied.

As Michel guts the chicken and starts cooking dinner—a simple Acadian stew called Frico—I keep him company in the kitchen, silently reviewing my performance. I imagine I smell of blood and keep seeing fresh drops of it on my trousers and shoes. Michel criticizes my technique but gives me high marks for "empathy." "Squeamishness" would be a better word. It is clear to me that I was trying to spare myself, not the chicken; my hesitation only caused it to suffer more. Through the window I see Brendan and Michel's daughter Mathilde, playing with the entrails, which they have dumped on the grass.

A week later, I visit Michel to say good-bye before leaving the island. He greets me warmly. "I sometimes make a mess of it myself," he confesses. He hands me a gift: a small oil painting he made of one of his roosters under a full moon.

Cold Turkey

31

I HAVE BEEN READING Nathaniel Hawthorne's account of his stint alone with his five-year-old son, "Twenty Days with Julian and Little Bunny, By Papa." It's August 1851. Hawthorne is in his late forties. Within hours of his wife's departure, he complains that he can't "write, read, think, or even sleep [during the day] so constant are [my son's] appeals to me." Later, he writes that his son's "continually thrusting" words "smash every attempt at reflection into a thousand fragments. . . . He has deafened and confounded me with his interminable babble. . . . Was ever man before so be-pelted with a child's talk as I am?"

I understand where he's coming from. My wife is away on a rare trip, and our son Brendan and I circle each other with apprehension. Brendan is four years old and has never spent twenty-four hours apart from his mother, let alone two weeks. It has been billed as "special time with Daddy," but neither of us is fooled. I'm still a wild card in Brendan's eyes. Our time together has been sporadic, consisting of raucous, happy sessions that seem divorced from the real business of our lives. When they're over, we're both apt to feel mildly relieved. Now we're thrown on each other, cold turkey.

As it happens, we needn't be so concerned. After a painless first night, Brendan is exhilarated. "I don't miss Mommy one bit," he says with amazement. All day he performs daredevil feats I have never seen him try before—walking on narrow ledges, hanging from metal bars, flourishing his arms like a trapeze artist, laughing wildly.

At bathtime he insists on a shower, though he has been violently against such a thing until now. "Is the water too hot?" I ask. "No. Make it hotter!" I worry that these are reckless acts of despair, but he seems genuinely euphoric, racing naked around the apartment, waving a wooden sword. He orders me to kidnap his stuffed chimpanzee and cook it. When I'm about to dig into my "meal," he leaps on me from behind. "Take your hands off him! I'm his father!" An aura of savage hilarity surrounds our first days.

His enthusiasm has a drawback, however. I've given up any hope of writing, but must I relinquish freedom of thought as well? Apparently so. Brendan is in the grip of a mania to turn every notion into words, and those words into action—a three-step process that takes place with molecular speed. When I beg him to give me a break, he slaps his forehead as if to say, "I can't believe what's happening myself." It would be useless, and possibly cruel, to try to stop him. He obviously can't help himself.

"Pretend that a pirate is disguised as your son," he says breathlessly. "When your real son comes you don't believe it's him. You think he's the pirate."

"What do I do?" I ask.

"You kill him. Then you find out he's your son. You're very sad. But he comes alive again."

His uninhibited plot twists make me question my own inventions, which seem torpid and over-cerebral by comparison. If I could combine the swashbuckler with Greek tragedy and Restoration farce, as Brendan appears to have done, I'd have a story worth pursuing. But my mind doesn't work that way anymore, if it ever did. Under his flood of language I become docile, dazed. I finally accept that I have no choice but to surrender. By the end of a week I'm following him around like an anxious valet.

At bedtime I get the chance to make up my own story without interference. A man lives with a family of monkeys. He loves the monkeys but he can't talk to them, he needs the company of another human being. So he goes off to find one. . . . At this point Brendan forbids me to continue. He detects an unsettling parallel in my story: the monkeys are him, I am the man. Bored with him, I take off to find someone I enjoy more. His face contorts into an expression of misery. Tears stream down his cheeks. I immediately adjust the plot line: the man doesn't abandon his monkeys; a companion comes to them, a woman. The monkeys greet her happily. The family is complete. Brendan grudgingly accepts this version and falls into a heavy sleep. I lie awake wondering how I could have misjudged my audience so badly.

Struggling to keep up with him, I begin to doubt whether I have what it takes for this job. My first son, Aaron, is older than Brendan by twenty-four years. I was twenty-one when he was born. When I look at young fathers, I see myself as I was back then—instinctual, ignorant, physically sure. I remember the vague condescension I sometimes felt toward middle-aged parents, stopping to rest on park benches, while I ran with my son till he was too exhausted to go on, then ostentatiously carried him home on my shoulders. Now I'm one of those depleted fathers, catching my breath with my hands on my knees. Aaron, when he visits, pokes fun at my attempts to keep pace with Brendan. There may be a trace of sibling rivalry in this; beneath his good-natured taunts, I hear him saying to me, "I had your best years."

Two nights before his mother is due to return, Brendan climbs into bed with me. "I dreamt I flew out of Mommy's arms."

"Was it scary?" I ask.

"Of course not. I was flying."

The next morning, he announces that he is frightened of "nothing in the whole world." It's crushingly hot outside, even at 8 a.m. On our street a fire hydrant is shooting water. Two boys throw a third into the spray, which is so powerful it pins him briefly against a car. The car's burglar alarm starts quacking. The boy ducks out of the deluge, soaked to the bone. A fire truck drives the wrong way down the street, its horn blaring. It stops at the hydrant. A fireman jumps out and closes the plug with an official-looking wrench. As soon as the truck leaves, a shirtless man with an identical wrench starts the water gushing again. Everyone cheers. A delivery boy on a bicycle gets sprayed. More cheers. Passing cars slow down to take advantage of the free wash. Brendan is riveted, thrilled, as if a new level of existence has burst to life in front of his eyes. For the first time in two weeks he is at a loss for words.

En route to the airport the next day, I ask him what he'll do when he sees Mommy. "Cut her head off," he answers.

When she comes through the gate, however, he runs into her arms and won't let go of her.

"I love you more than Daddy," he whispers, a remark I'm not intended to hear.

I feel a jealous stab. Our days alone together begin their automatic slide into memory. I already think of it as an idyllic time.

Cardiac Arrest

32

CURT, DISTRESSED, my mother's husband, Marvin, phones me with the news. "They're saying that your mother had a heart attack. We're in the emergency room. St. Luke's Hospital, on the East Side."

By the time I arrive she has been transferred to the cardiac unit, where I find her in a small, untidy room on the fifth floor. A computer screen above the bed tracks her blood pressure and heartbeat. Several bags of IV fluid complete the picture. But my mother is sitting up in bed, alert and sardonic, wondering what all the fuss is about and lamenting that she has nothing to read. A thin, elegant woman, she seems offended by the frayed gown that she has been given to wear. Compensating for this indignity are the nurses who marvel at how young she looks at eighty-two years of age.

"I feel indestructible," she announces, discounting the paralyzing chest pains that prompted Marvin to bring her to the emergency room. She dismisses as "inaccurate" the results of preliminary tests that suggest her life may be in danger.

My brothers Ben and Robert arrive with their wives. We greet each other warmly and sidle around the room like passengers crammed into the compartment of a train. Marvin sits in a steel chair, struggling with our competing claim on his wife. Rejecting the somber mood, my mother repeats a joke she heard at her weekly bridge game. On his eightieth birthday, a widower is offered the gift of "super sex" with a prostitute. He hears "soup or sex," and gratefully opts for the former. We sons smile uneasily, while Marvin laughs and tenderly strokes her hand.

A short, powerful, fireplug of a man, Marvin is a retired plumber who, for sixty years, repaired oil furnaces in Brooklyn. Less than two years ago, we looked on in amazement as, clutching each other's hands, he and our mother recited their vows under a rented wedding canopy in the living room of her apartment. They immediately embarked on a life of abandon, as if racing against time—drinking daily martinis, taking road trips for the hell of it, eating tacos, Big Macs, fried chicken, and thick mail-order steaks from Nebraska. They can't bear to be apart. By comparison, my own marriage and those of my brothers seem predictable and worn.

In the hospital, we scold her for her reckless behavior. We are the cholesterol-fearing sons. "You can't keep living like this," we say. "You have to think of your health, your future."

Do I detect a subtle smirk of defiance at our warning? As we say goodnight, she asks Marvin to remember to bring her perfume in the morning.

"You don't need perfume in the hospital," he answers.

"Wrong, my love. The hospital is where you need it most."

The following day, the stream of visitors continues. Our voices drown out the groans of the woman in the next bed, four feet away, separated from us by a curtain. The nurses rush to and fro, responding to the life-and-death struggles that seem to be taking place in every corner of the ward except ours. I worry that we are too loud, but the nurses are louder, teasing one another, tacitly encouraging our chatter.

My mother's hairdresser bursts in, with six rings on his fingers and a thick crucifix around his neck. He spends an hour complaining about the crankiness of his lover, compliments the cardiologist for her "lovely maternity dress," though she isn't pregnant, kisses my mother with tears in his eyes, and dashes off. My eldest brother, Ben, reads her vital signs, which crawl across the computer screen like stock quotes. Danny, the youngest, a doctor himself, phones from Seattle to talk about her "inverted Q waves," her troubling enzyme levels, and her left anterior descending artery, which he suspects is the source of her pain. Robert comes hopping in on crutches. He broke his foot running across the street that morning. I wonder if this is an expression of sympathy with my mother, with whom he is especially close. I remember the spectacular accidents, such as falling from balconies, that he was prone to as a boy. Laughing lightly at himself, Robert says, "See what I go through for you." And her status as the adored matriarch is sealed.

It is time for her angiogram, the moment of truth. Various dyes are to be injected into her heart through a catheter, lighting it up like a video game so that all will be revealed. On the phone my mother sounds anxious. When I return to the hospital she is in the midst of the procedure, at the cardio-surgery center on the eleventh floor.

I ride up and wait for her. Other families are waiting too, hushed and exhausted. An hour passes without word. I am restless and frightened for her. I try not to imagine the worst. Sun pours through the long, south-facing windows, while on the walls hang the poster of a lush Van Huysum still life, and Sisley's soothing "Effets de Neige." A carefully thought-out decor. I remember a friend who underwent cancer treatment in another Manhattan hospital. "Without exception," she told me, "the staff glowed with health. The message was: this is a place of vitality, of life. But looking at them I felt like a hungry person peering through a restaurant window."

After two hours, the surgeon emerges. "Congratulations. She's completely clear. No damage whatsoever. If the hearts of all my patients looked like this, I'd be out of business." He slips me his card, as if tipping a maitre d'hotel, and disappears again behind the forbidding steel doors. My mother is smiling from her gurney, wearing lipstick and rouge, perfectly applied.

The next day she is discharged, and I visit her at her apartment. Marvin is mixing celebratory martinis. They are relaxed enough to bicker about my mother's housekeeper, the one point of contention between them. Though forty years younger than my mother, the housekeeper constantly complains of pain—in her stomach, her legs, her head—that prevents her from exerting herself. To make things easier for her, my mother cleans the apartment herself the day before the housekeeper is due to arrive. Marvin can't bear it. He wants to fire her, but my mother refuses to let him. At the end of his rope, he offers me the story for "a sure bestseller": the husband plots the housekeeper's death, a perfect murder. My mother teasingly weighs in with an alternative plot: the housekeeper drives the husband insane.

Both scenarios, I notice, have the same ending. The wife lives happily ever after.

33

WHEN HE WAS A U.S. ARMY SURGEON in the South Pacific during the Second World War, my Uncle Nat circumcised his entire battalion. "I was killing time, waiting to be shipped to Saipan where the action was. I designed a clamp for the procedure, which the boys built for me in the shop." I picture him in a modern variant of the biblical story in which David brings King Saul the foreskins of a hundred Philistines to prove his prowess.

Nat had entered Harvard in 1932 at the age of fourteen, the youngest in his class and one of only two Jews to be admitted that year, thanks to Harvard's strict quota. I was familiar with his stories of humiliation as an undergraduate and wondered if this alpha marking of his battalion was a belated form of revenge. Or maybe he had been seeking to neutralize his own mark of separation by inscribing it on everyone else. I reminded him that Jews first took up circumcision as a means of belonging, imitating the initiation practice of the Egyptian priestly caste; it was only later, in Europe, that it became an emblem of the pariah.

Nat dismissed such notions. "It wasn't obligatory. The men volunteered. The only incentive I offered was two days off from drill duty. Somehow they got it in their heads that the operation would make them more potent."

Today, Nat's chief regret is that he neglected to obtain a patent for his clamp. He would have made a fortune. After the war, newborn males were automatically circumcised in America's hospitals, on the assumption that it prevented genital infection and reduced the risk of cervical cancer in women. Until then, Jews had been the only people who circumcised infants—on the eighth day after birth, according to rabbinical law, since the boy's sacrificial blood must flow only after the mother's "tainted" blood had ceased to. The American Academy of Pediatrics recommends circumcising babies twelve to twenty-four hours after they are born. "Tighten the thumbscrew to crush the foreskin between the bell and the base plate; then cut the foreskin using a scalpel blade," reads a current instruction manual for physicians.

The universalizing of an ancient tribal ritual, on purely medical grounds, is one of the curiosities of postwar America. Leonard Glick, in his book *Marked in Your Flesh*, says that Jewish doctors were especially persuasive about the benefits of the procedure. Maybe my uncle had been one of its promoters. It marked the reversal of popular views about circumcision in Europe where, before the war, the practice had been widely seen as unsanitary. It was believed, among other things, that the ritual circumciser, or *mohel*, transmitted syphilis to the baby. By uniformly branding the flesh of young males on its maternity wards, America's pediatricians appear to have achieved the assimilation of the Jews.

In ancient times, it fell to the father to do the job on his son himself, driving home the idea that masculinity belonged to God or to the priests who spoke for him. For Freud, this was proof of the violence of the father who crashes in on the paradise of mother and child. Elsewhere, he speculates that circumcision is a substitute for castration which "during the human family's primeval period . . . used to be carried out by a jealous and cruel father upon growing boys."

His anthropology seems shaky. It is more likely that it was a replacement for the actual killing of babies to propitiate the gods. Such sacrifice was common in Canaan, as the story of Isaac and Abraham attests. In a scene in Exodus, God, fed up with Moses's reluctance to do his bidding, resolves to kill him. Moses's wife Zipporah hastily cuts off their son's foreskin and smears Moses with the blood, thus performing the sacrifice that appeases God.

In 1975, when my son was born, his Cuban and black crib mates were circumcised as a matter of course. When it was Aaron's turn, his mother declined the offer with a wave of her hand. I let it slide, wondering if we weren't, by some irony of history, imposing an unwanted distinction on him. Without the blessing of a mohel, I reasoned, circumcision is religiously meaningless. And since I wasn't observant enough to engage one, why subject Aaron to unnecessary pain? My first wife and her family seemed to me a jubilant atheist clan, liberated from history, as I saw it, while I was hung up on a collection of myths, expectations, and recorded deeds.

One day while visiting my parents, I was changing Aaron's diaper in the closet. My grandmother caught a glimpse of him naked, and spent the rest of the day in her bedroom, weeping. Afterward, watching him bathe, the line from Genesis came to mind: "He who fails to circumcise the flesh of his foreskin has broken my covenant and shall be cut off from his kin." Then came what seemed like a sign from Jehovah: Aaron's pediatrician informed me that, owing to a rare condition, circumcision was necessary for medical reasons. "A one-in-a-million occurrence," he said. I was off the hook.

Seven years ago, when my second son was born, I felt the familiar lurch of ambivalence. On the ward circumcision was less popular than it had been and, with the doctor's encouragement, we said no to the scalpel.

When one of my brothers heard of our decision, he was indignant. "Didn't you learn your lesson with Aaron?"

I argued that the mandate to circumcise was from the "P" or priestly version of the Bible. It had been written more than three hundred years after the original and was shoehorned into the text along with various dietary laws. "The covenant asks for blood, but does it have to come from a newborn's genitals?"

My brother was unimpressed. To him, I am the worst traitor: a nonbeliever who was brought up to believe. "It's in the Torah," he said.

I persisted: "Surely one's affiliation is defined by more than a scar?"

I meant to cite Tolstoy's dictum that there is only one aristocracy, the aristocracy of the spirit, but realized that I was inadvertently echoing the apostle Paul who declared that, for the "new" Jew, faith was inscribed on the heart, not the flesh.

I'm waiting for another sign from Jehovah.

The Importance of Pronouns

MY WIFE, PAT, brought a friend from work home for dinner. Georgina was her name, and when she entered the apartment I felt a potent mix of fascination, awe, and incomprehension. She was in her late twenties, with bobbed reddish hair, pale blanched-looking skin, and a body that had been scoured of its maleness by hormone infusions and sex reassignment surgery. Yet it was obvious at a glance that she was not a woman.

Plump, delicate, and sublimely self-conscious, she made herself immediately at home, uncorking the bottle of cider she had brought and toasting us with a patient smile. "To new friends." Pat and Georgina settled themselves on the couch and fell into an animated conversation that seemed to be the continuation of one they had been having before they arrived.

I went into the kitchen, poured my cider into the sink, and made myself a bourbon. When I returned, I overheard Pat excitedly describing her days as a street performer when she was around Georgina's age. This is the part of Pat's life that I am least familiar with, the part that had thrived before we met and faded gradually during the years of our marriage, the part that I stripped away from her—or so I suspected she believed—just as Georgina's masculinity had been stripped away, without entirely disappearing.

Pat rarely talked to me about that time of her life, but with Georgina the stories flowed out of her with spontaneous ease: the communion with the other performers, the bewilderment or delight of passersby, the hassles from the cops. It was as if she shared with Georgina some drastic social impulse that I was too square to understand.

I sat down in a chair across from them and forced my way into the conversation. "Pat's performances were mesmerizing, before she disbanded her dance company," I said.

"Oh, I don't doubt it," purred Georgina.

She looked oddly ageless in her white button-down shirt, intelligent and content, with a touch of smugness, justifiable perhaps in one who had partially succeeded in overturning one of Nature's most intractable laws.

She turned back to Pat, encouraging her to go on. I interrupted them again, bombarding Georgina with questions as if I were interviewing her for a job. "Where did you grow up?" (Eugene, Oregon.) "What did your father do?" (He was a lawyer for a grass-seed company.) Almost without thinking, I took my notepad from my pocket and started jotting her answers down.

Pat angrily ordered me to put the notepad away. "You're embarrassing me, Michael."

"I just want to get his language right," I explained.

"Her language," Georgina corrected me. "Pronouns are very important," she added sternly. "Some genderqueers I know prefer no pronouns at all."

Pat gave me a scalding look and marched into the kitchen to prepare dinner.

I asked Georgina if my curiosity made her uncomfortable.

She smiled calmly, sipping her cider. "Mildly so. But don't let it stop you. It's obviously what you need to do." My blunt interest seemed to amuse her, as if she too thought of herself as exotic, and enjoyed the idea that I was struggling to understand her. She informed me that she was a polyamorist, a vegetarian, a transgender activist, and a student of the works of Lacan, "even though Lacan would have regarded someone like me as psychotic. He's about reading symbols, and so am I."

She had recently finished writing a novel about "Christian fascist fanatics," whose plot to poison America is thwarted by an alliance of lesbians, genderqueers, runaways, and outlaw artists. "The writing is terrible, but otherwise it's not bad." The story was inspired by an anarchist riot in Eugene in 1999, when nineteen people wearing black masks were arrested after smashing the display windows of Starbucks and Gap stores.

"I got away," said Georgina. "I'm an ideologue, if you haven't figured it out already, an Anarcho-Marxist, not an Anarcho-Primitivist as I started out to be. The Primitivists want to abolish all forms of civilization. I allow that some aspects of civilization are okay."

She told me of her father's death from prostate cancer when he was "about as old as you."

"You've filled yourself with the hormones that suppress what killed him," I said, referring to the testosterone that Georgina had taken such pains to eradicate from her system.

She looked at me sharply and then lowered her eyes. "He was the only one in my family who supported my decision to become a transwoman."

Under the influence of a Buddhist teacher, Georgina was pondering whether to take a "chastity vow." I wondered if this provided a clue to her true aspiration: Buddhism proposes a state in which there are no pronouns, because there is no "I." Masculine and feminine are just illusions in a world that is nothing more than a dream. Jan Morris, in her book *Conundrum*, writes that she equated her transsexual impulses with "the idea of soul. . . . I was aiming at a more divine condition. . . . To me gender is not physical at all . . . it concerned not my apparatus but my self." Of sexual intercourse, Morris writes, "I wanted to be rid of it."

Maybe Georgina had similar ideas about her transformation. But if this were primarily a spiritual quest, why did it require the wrenching physical ordeal of hormones and the surgeon's knife?

At dinner, Georgina was childlike and giddy, poring over the crossword puzzle from our copy of the *New York Times*, happily involving Pat and me in the clues. She announced that she was a Taurus. "My girlfriend's a Scorpio. We're irresistible opposites. A perfect match."

I told her that I was a Scorpio too, and to Pat's astonishment Georgina embraced me.

After she left, however, Pat scolded me again for my rudeness. "You were hell bent on turning her into some kind of specimen for your observation. She's not a novelty act,

Michael. If you wanted to take notes you could at least have had the courtesy to leave the room and do it in private."

When I asked her what she thought had motivated Georgina to do what she did to herself, she said, "It's the ultimate freedom. I am what I say I am, not what I was born. For Georgina it's a political statement, a position. I just hope she doesn't grow up to regret it."

She demanded to know why I had barged into their conversation and taken Georgina over for myself. "It was as if you wanted to keep us apart."

I tried to explain the impact of her presence. "It threatened to pry open an old rift between us."

Pat laughed at me in disbelief. "I can assure you, Michael, that was all in your mind."

Ideal Love

35

AN ACQUAINTANCE, Barbara Foster, phones to invite me to the monthly meeting of her "polyamory group" in Greenwich Village. "We believe in multiple love relationships," she explains. "An extended family where everything's above board—you're fully aware of your partner's lovers, and he knows all about yours. No cheating, no broken trust, which, as you know, is what causes love to crumble."

I pull *The Kreutzer Sonata* from my shelf, Tolstoy's diatribe against sex, to read on the subway ride downtown. The narrator, Pozdnyshev, mocks the notion that "spiritual affinity" is the basis of marriage. "Is it because of unity of ideals that people go to bed together?" he asks sarcastically. He can't bear the fact that, duped by sexual attraction, he convinced himself he had fallen in love. When attraction ends, contempt takes over, lasting until the couple's last miserable breath. Yet we "go to the grave believing we have lived perfectly normal and happy lives!" cries Pozdnyshev. To protect the "purity" of ideal love, Pozdnyshev proposes chastity in marriage.

The meeting is to take place at the Gay, Lesbian, Bisexual, and Transgender Community Center, a former elementary school on West 13th Street, filled with concealed staircases and unexpected wings. "We're just renting space here," a polyamorist hastens to inform me. "For the most part, they're completely confused about who we are."

About forty people have gathered in a room tucked away in a remote corner of the third floor. An air-conditioner rattles loudly. Strips of black duct tape keep the carpet from coming apart. Our chairs are arranged in a circle, like in nursery school.

I find Barbara, who hands me a book she co-wrote entitled *Three in Love: Ménages à Trois from Ancient to Modern Times*. The other authors are her husband and the third member of their ménage. "I lived it," she says with disarming intensity. Among the threesomes she profiles are Joseph and Magda Goebbels and Lida Baarova; Charles Parnell and Kitty and Willy O'Shea; Jack Kerouac and Neal and Carolyn Cassady; and Superman, Clark Kent, and Lois Lane.

It occurs to me that the characters in *The Kreutzer Sonata* also make up a ménage à trois. When Pozdnyshev beholds his wife playing duets with his rival, he is captivated by "her fascinating, abhorrent face . . . her perfectly melting mood, her tenderly pathetic and blissful smile." Pozdnyshev is excited by the music as well. "In consequence of my jealousy, there passed between them a kind of electric current." To deny his rival the satisfaction of knowing how threatened he feels, Pozdnyshev invites him to come and play again with his wife. "I was aware that I could not control that body of hers." Out of his mind with jealousy, he murders her with a curved Damascus dagger.

At eight o'clock sharp, the featured speaker bursts into the room. She is Nan Wise, Certified Relationship and Alternative Lovestyles Specialist, and Happiness Coach. Tall, voluptuous, with long coppery hair, she looks as if she has stepped out of the pages of a Robert Crumb cartoon. To complete the picture, she has brought along her lover, or her "secondary relationship," as the polyamorists would call him. Her husband couldn't make it but, she assures us, "he's poly, too."

"Languaging is of critical importance," Nan says. We are immediately bombarded with made-up words, apparently meant to lend a sociological aura to the movement. A heavyset man wants to know how to present his polyamorous desire to his monogamous girlfriend.

"The dreaded poly/mono dilemma!" Nan cries. "To lead this life successfully, you need advanced skill-sets. They can be learned. But they require commitment. Sacrifice, in some cases. Maturity. Work."

The couple sitting next to me clutch each other's hands, like nervous passengers on a plane.

The polyamorist's ultimate goal is to reach the state of "compersion," where jealousy is transcended and "one finds pleasure in the pleasure of his lover with another"—a variation, perhaps, of Pozdnyshev's ideal love. The ability to negotiate is paramount. "Advance-skill polys can cut a relationship deal in three to five minutes," Nan says. The guidelines are simple: "win/win or no deal."

An older, bearded man briefly takes the floor. He claims to have been a contented polyamorist for more than thirty years. "I'm uncomfortable with the word *compromise*, with its negative connotations of giving something up." All agree that *collaborate* should replace it as the favored term. Another participant reports that, after they went poly, his wife of twenty years left him. He seems morose and stung, but sympathy for his plight is measured. He has failed to reach compersion. However, more bruised feelings from members of the audience come to light. A young woman worries about maintaining primary status with her main lover. "I don't want to be demoted to number two or three." Another complains of being stuck at a low rung on the ladder. "I feel like a mistress. I mean, what the hell am I doing this for?"

Maybe a change of language would ease her discomfort. "'Primary' could be 'principal,' and the rest could be called 'satellites,'" suggests the bearded man. "It's less hierarchal."

Wise's secondary pipes up with advice of his own: "Life is fluid and love even more so. Today's secondary may move to the top, while the primary may be struck off the list entirely." He glances pleadingly at Nan, who ignores him. As the meeting breaks up, a "cuddle party" is announced for next week—"for people who want more touch in their lives without it leading to sex or rejection."

An outspoken member of the group, Birgitte, invites a few friends to her apartment across the street, and she allows me to tag along. As she unlocks the door, two eager identical miniature dogs greet her, and Birgitte, large-bodied and with a queenly demeanor, scoops them up in her arms.

The apartment is stacked with her Michel Basquiat–inspired paintings. Each canvas has its title scrawled across the top. "She was his flavor of the month," reads one. "He fucked her brains out," goes another. In her day job, Birgitte works as a makeup artist. "I did Condoleezza Rice for a television appearance," she tells me.

Standing against the wall I spot a large canvas, called "He's her twin." A woman and a man are holding hands. Each has a real dagger sticking out of his large, papier-mâché heart.

36

AT A DINNER RECENTLY I was sitting next to a French woman named Solange who had just moved to New York. She wanted to know if I was familiar with "the early twentieth-century American novelist Levenson." She couldn't remember the writer's first name nor how to spell his last name, nor the title of the novel that in every other respect "has stayed in my head for years."

I wondered if she was thinking of Abraham Cahan's novel *The Rise of David Levinsky*—about a self-made garment-industry tycoon—and had confused the name in the title with that of the author.

"No, no," said Solange in her heavily accented English. "This is the story of a miserable marriage. I've been asking Americans about Levenson since I arrived here, but no one I talk to has any idea who he is."

She informed me that in France the novel was known as a critique of American moral hypocrisy. "Antonin Artaud admired it. So did Gide. It's still in print. I wish I could tell you more."

The following morning I did a Web search, and only one remotely viable candidate turned up: Sam Levenson, the stand-up comedian and writer who lived down the street from me in Rockaway when I was a boy. He was our neighborhood celebrity, with his own radio show on CBS. Among Levenson's books in my family library were *Anything But Money*, *Sex and the Single Child*, and *You Don't Have to Be in Who's Who to Know What's What*. He had grown up in an East Harlem tenement, and the basis of his comedy routine was the anxiety that accompanied his generation's swift rise from poverty to the middle class. According to Levenson, Freud and the new "Kindergarchy," in which children were the tribal rulers, had destroyed the natural order. His lost mythic hero was "Mama" who could "thread a needle in the dark with one hand, tie a knot with her teeth, and chop meat with her free hand." Mama hated dirt and tore through her children's scalps "with a horse brush soaked in naphtha soap"; to kill lice she added kerosene. I fondly remember his story about the time he brought a narcissus bulb home from school as a boy. "An uncle grated it and ate it with sardines." Could this man have written the desperate novel about marriage that Solange described?

When I was eight or nine, I broke Levenson's parlor window while playing stoop ball. He rushed out of the house, a round-faced man wearing a bow tie and thick wire-rimmed glasses, followed by his tall, regal wife whom I had often heard him describe as "my childhood sweetheart." I could sense that he felt obligated to give me a lecture that I wouldn't forget, and at the same time I could make out his rising amusement.

After showing me the damage I had caused, he held up my ball, led me into the kitchen and chopped it in half with a cleaver.

The next step in my investigation was to go to Esther Schor, a professor of English at Princeton, and she guessed right away that the writer was Ludwig Lewisohn. "Spoken with a French accent the name could easily sound like Levenson," she explained. Schor hadn't read him and couldn't think of anyone she knew who had. "All I can tell you is that he published forty books, most of them between the First and Second World Wars, and that he had a homosexual affair with George Viereck, who spent four years in a federal prison for conspiring with the Nazis. Princeton owns their love letters."

Lewisohn's affair with Viereck took place while they were both students at Columbia, around 1904. Viereck was the one to break it off, at exactly the moment when Lewisohn's graduate thesis was rejected and two of his professors warned him that no American university would hire a Jew to teach English.

Shortly thereafter, Lewisohn married a woman twenty years older than he was and already a grandmother. He wrote of the marriage in *The Case of Mr. Crump*, the novel, I was able to ascertain with a phone call to Solange, that she had spoken to me about at dinner.

I tracked down a copy of the novel, which arrived in the mail with a blurb on the cover from Sigmund Freud—"an incomparable masterpiece"—and a preface, written in 1931, by Thomas Mann. Mann's cryptic praise for the book only served to sharpen my expectations. "It is more and less than a novel," Mann writes, "it is concrete and undreamed reality and its artistic silence seems . . . like a cry."

The book's obscurity in the United States seemed to be mainly the fault of its unusual publishing history. In 1926,

Edward Titus, an American patron of avant-garde literature, brought out an English edition of *The Case of Mr. Crump* in Paris. The threat of a libel suit from Lewisohn's estranged wife, however, prevented the book from being sold in the U.S. until 1947. When it did appear in America, reviews were respectful, and the novel slipped into oblivion, except for an abridged mass paperback version, retitled *The Tyranny of Sex*, which sold more than a million copies, but did nothing to help the novel's literary reputation.

Reading it, I realized at once that it was Lewisohn's swollen late-Victorian style that had doomed the novel's prospects in America. "Their feeble bumptiousness only revealed more grotesquely their inner supineness," goes a typical sentence. Several references are made to the protagonist's "heavenly intoxicating ichor." When Lewisohn breaks free of this tone, a jarring realism takes over, driven by Crump's infernally detailed hatred of his wife. I understood what had lingered in Solange's head—the kind of to-the-death animus you find in Strindberg. "Did he have to sit still and let the mud of her seep and splash and ooze and poison and choke all things decent and kindly and not ignoble and of good report?" Lewisohn's bad luck was to be born fifteen years before the Lost Generation, whose writers would make his prose instantly obsolete.

I felt disappointed, and oddly sad for the forty books Lewisohn had published: fifteen works of fiction, and several volumes of autobiography and criticism, as well as essays against the stranglehold of the Anglo-Saxon intellectual aristocracy, as Lewisohn saw it, and the sexual repression of puritanism. His was a consciousness that painstakingly recorded itself, and then disappeared.

A couple of days later, one of Sam Levenson's books arrived in the mail. *In One Era Out the Other*, it's called.

"Everything I Hate in Fiction"

THE NEWS OF TED SOLOTAROFF'S DEATH last month* at the age of eighty brought me back to my teenage years in the late 1960s, when I would read the first issues of *New American Review*, the magazine Solotaroff edited, while standing at the bookstore where they had pride of place on the display tables near the front.

He had the ingenious idea of publishing the magazine as a mass-market paperback, which gave it a relaxed, deceptively arbitrary air. It didn't go in much for polemic, as *Commentary* or *Partisan Review* did, nor agitprop and Beat erotica like the *Evergreen Review*, its main rival. *New American Review* had a subtle ear-to-the-ground feeling; you read it the way you might eavesdrop at an interesting party, hoping to edge your way into the conversation. Solotaroff was constantly

*Solotaroff died on August 8, 2008.

scrambling for new financial backers, insisting, against mounting evidence to the contrary, that there was a large audience for this kind of open-ended literary review. He published portions of *Portnoy's Complaint* before it became a novel, and provided early glimpses of Kate Millett's *Sexual Politics*. E. L. Doctorow's *Ragtime* was serialized in the *NAR*, and in 1973 it offered "Cadillac Flambé" by Ralph Ellison, billed as a chapter from Ellison's "almost completed" second novel (it would, of course, never be finished).

After a few years, Solotaroff dropped the "New" from the title, and in 1977 he announced that the magazine had run its course. It had become "a kind of holding action instead of pioneering," he said. "You pretty much work out your ideas in ten years, and also go through your emotions."

In the early 1980s, my novel was recommended to Solotaroff, who was then an editor at Harper & Row, by one of his writers. I heard from him after only a week. A letter in the mailbox: "This manuscript represents everything I hate in fiction. Good luck trying to find it a home." It was like having the host of the party throw a drink in your face the instant you walk through the door. The friend who had recommended it seemed as flustered as I was by his response, tainted by association, fearing perhaps that some flaw in her taste had been exposed. I suspected that Solotaroff had elaborated on his intense dislike of my manuscript, but she didn't want to discuss it, probably wishing to spare me further pain. "You've written a book powerful enough to disturb him," she said, offering as good a backhanded compliment as I've ever had. "His usual rejection note says, 'Thank you, but it's not my cup of tea.' You've served him tea with poison."

For months I tried to puzzle out what he meant by "everything I hate in fiction." Was it style, the story, or something as uncorrectable as the essence of the writer himself? Maybe it was the volatile, self-dramatizing father in the novel that put him off, or the politics of one of his sons—a radical idealist with a delicate constitution, a martyr complex, and a mystical streak that seemed at odds with Solotaroff's own sensible view of the world. I thought of trying to make an appointment to ask him to explain, but what was the point of provoking another insult? I would look like just another aggrieved writer.

I looked for clues in Solotaroff's book of essays, *The Red Hot Vacuum*, a collection of pieces on the writing of the 1960s. The "vacuum," as he explained it, was created by empty literary posturing, "a kind of feverish present-mindedness and self-absorption" among American writers, "a passionate style coupled with a vacancy of content." I sensed an ambivalence in his taste, a feeling of nostalgia for the radical formalities of the *Partisan Review* crowd, and a vague disapproval for the new writing he had helped to launch. With its complicated, immigrant-minded fathers and their sons, my novel must have seemed old hat to him, a story of Jewish marginality that, in America at least, was passé.

In the mid-1990s, however, Solotaroff published a piece about the irony of trying to write a book that as an editor he would have rejected as too difficult to sell. He had left his publishing job to work on an "oft-told story of two immigrant East European families and of growing up Jewish in America in the 1930s and 40s. I retired because I couldn't afford to have one side of my mind saying to the other, 'Come on, Ted, who cares anymore about this personal and dated stuff?' Or, 'Who is going to buy this book?'—the leading question of the career I had just left."

After hearing of his death, I picked up the book in question, a memoir of his childhood called *Truth Comes in Blows*. It's a boy's view of a tyrannical and violently unpredictable father. Reading it, I was amazed at the similarities between his upbringing and mine, despite the twenty-five-year difference in our ages. Solotaroff might have recognized this similarity too when rejecting my novel. His father, Ben, was in the plate-glass business, cutting glass in his unheated shop, and carefully removing broken storefront windows so as to preserve the usable remnant, much the way my father salvaged old metal in his scrap yard. "My feelings for him were like a high-speed elevator, either inert or else shooting up to rage or down to pity," he writes.

Ben Solotaroff resented what little he gave to his son, worked himself to the bone, and felt eternally shortchanged. "I'm going to break your spirit for good," he told him. He splashed out on extravagant solo vacations, and took the tender part of the steak at dinner, or the breast of the chicken, "then pushed the platter over to Mom to cut up what was left. 'Eat bread, kids,' he'd say. 'Don't fill up on meat.'"

In order to break away and become "anything worthwhile," Ted would have to "squeeze the slave out of myself, as Chekhov put it, drop by drop." When he found his father's body in his house in New Jersey, he thought: "The death I had wished for . . . had come to pass. The rest was just a corpse I had to do something about."

I wondered if the character he disliked most in my novel was not the radical son, but his conservative brother who had done what neither Ted nor I had done—that is, dutifully gone into his father's business.

About five years ago I met Solotaroff at a party. He seemed withdrawn and tense. I mentioned, casually, the rejection note. "Twenty years ago, you say?" He didn't remember it. "Maybe it made you stronger. The name of the game is endurance. I've seen a lot of writers drop away after a few decent stories and disappear."

I HAVE BEEN READING Aharon Appelfeld's gripping and elusive memoir, *The Story of a Life*, about his childhood during the Holocaust. Appelfeld escaped from a Nazi work camp at the age of seven and survived alone for six years in the Ukrainian woods, scavenging for food and occasionally doing chores for peasant farmers in exchange for a place to sleep. He was able to pass as one of them in the halting Ukrainian he had picked up, explaining, falsely, that his parents had been killed in an air raid.

"I've written more than twenty books about those years, but sometimes it seems as though I haven't yet begun to describe them," Appelfeld writes. "For a child, memory is a reservoir that doesn't empty."

Yet he has never been able to write about the specifics of what happened or how. His attempts to do so have yielded "jumbled phrases, incorrect words, disjointed rhythm, weak or exaggerated characters."

I was midway through Appelfeld's book when news came of a Belgian woman living in Massachusetts who had fabricated a memoir of her childhood as a Jewish girl on the run in Europe during the Second World War. Reading Appelfeld's authentic story, I found myself thinking about the false one. *Misha: A Memoir of the Holocaust Years* was published eleven years ago by a small New England press, Mt. Ivy. It had a recommendation from Elie Wiesel, was translated into eighteen languages, and inspired an Italian opera. In January 2008, a movie based on the book, *Survivre avec les loups*, was released in France. In the story, seven-year-old Misha Defonseca treks from Brussels to the Ukraine in search of her deported parents. Along the way she makes a stop at the Warsaw Ghetto, which she leaves by climbing over a wall. She stabs and kills a Nazi when he tries to rape her, and is protected in her journey through the forest by a pack of wolves.

When some readers pointed to the book's inaccuracies (Misha's parents are taken away in the spring of 1940, for example, seventeen months before the deportation of Belgian Jews began) or questioned the plausibility of her charming tales about wolves, they were tarred as Holocaust deniers. The director of *Survivre avec les loups*, Vera Belmont, accused the doubters of being "exactly like people who doubt the existence of concentration camps. Everything that happened during the Holocaust is unbelievable and impossible to grasp." After learning that Misha Defonseca's real name was Monique De Wael, that she was a Catholic, and that she had confessed to making up the memoir, Belmont said, "No matter if it's true or not, it's a beautiful story."

De Wael for her part, blamed her publisher for talking her into putting out the book. "She made me believe, and I believed it," she said. "The story of Misha is not actual reality, but my reality, my way of surviving." She said that her parents were Belgian resistance fighters, killed by Nazis. "I always felt Jewish, always created a different life for myself, a life far from the people I hated."

The following day, March 4, the *New York Times* revealed another case of what Daniel Mendelsohn has called the "plagiarism of other people's trauma": a memoir by Margaret B. Jones entitled *Love and Consequences*. Jones presents herself as a "half-Native American, half-Caucasian" foster child who, with her possessions in a rubbish bag, was shunted from one miserable shelter to the next. At the age of eight she was given a permanent home with a woman called "Big Mom" and her black family in South Central Los Angeles during the most violent period of the 1980s gang wars. As with De Wael's fabrication, I was struck by the wealth of detail enveloping the author's soul-destroying childhood years. By contrast, Appelfeld's memoir is surrounded by a feeling of amnesia.

Reviewers marveled at "the bonds of love and loyalty" that Jones's story describes, and praised its "heart-tingling" qualities, its tenderness, lyricism, and "nurturer's point of view." But do violent death and grief really give rise to lyricism and heart-tingle? If unspeakable acts of abuse offer the victim the opportunity for a heightened experience of healing and stirring prose, then the society that abuses can't be all that bad. Maybe that's why readers and publishers seem to embrace victimhood as a peculiar privilege, a means to achieve emotional transcendence. The victim, like the sinner, is given a chance to be born again.

When Margaret Jones was confronted with the fact that she was really Margaret Seltzer, who grew up in a well-to-do suburb and attended a private Episcopal day school, she continued, like De Wael, to express her belief in the righteousness of her fantasy self. As the only "white girl" living in the ghetto with Big Mom, she enjoyed an irreproachable identity. "It was my opportunity to put a voice to those who people don't listen to," she said. "I just felt there was a good I could do, and there was no other way."

Appelfeld's memoir brought me back to the sanity of darkness. Neurologists have found that children don't have the capacity to create memory as adults do, and Appelfeld's struggle, as he recounts it, was to find words for the buried imprints of his childhood. "The cells of my body apparently remember more than my mind, which is supposed to remember," he writes. Places, individuals, specific events have been forgotten. Chronologies don't exist. Words are "pitiable . . . and easily distorted." The six years of war had seemed like a single night. "I had been by myself and hadn't spoken to anyone." After the war it was assumed he was mute. "But then I really was almost mute."

In Israel, where Appelfeld settled, people demanded testimonials and facts from the survivors, not poetry or stories. "Build and be rebuilt" was the national slogan in the 1950s. Stories that reached deeper could be tinged with a nostalgia for Europe that the new state was intent on erasing. Appelfeld's first attempts at writing were "like the howling of an abandoned animal who takes up his cries time and again with a wearying monotony." He was trying to draw out of himself what he desired to repress even further, a kind of soul language precise enough to transmit a measure of silence.

While I was talking to a friend about the book, he repeated a story that Appelfeld had told him. After the war, Appelfeld discovered that a man with his name had arrived in Israel from Europe. "Aharon went to the kibbutz where this Appelfeld was living and found his father on a ladder pruning an apple tree. They were so astonished that they were unable to speak to each other for months."

When asked why he hadn't put the story in his memoir, Appelfeld said he was afraid that if he did he would never write another word.

39

THE WRITING OF A MEMOIR is a tricky proposition, and not only because the form has been dragged through the mud by its own practitioners in recent years. Philip Roth's novel *The Counterlife* contains a passage about "the strange bind" in which the family members of a writer find themselves. "Their own material is articulated for them by someone else who, in his voracious, voyeuristic using-up of their lives, gets there first but doesn't always get it right."

Having written a memoir about my daughter Sally's manic breakdown, I've put my own family in this bind. So far, I've offered the manuscript to every principal character except Sally, seeking their consent, if not outright blessing. My emotionally troubled brother Steve waved it away without so much as a glance at the title. "Mikey, if you tell the truth about me, I don't want to read it."

Most of the others seemed to accept what I had written about them, though not without hints of resentment. Sally's mother, Robin, praised the book in a strained voice that concealed her objections. "What's the point of getting into it," she said when I assured her that I could still make changes. Pleased to be off the hook, I didn't press the matter further. It was naive of me to expect Robin to embrace my version of her, with its cold printed aura of the final word.

My present wife, Pat, also had complaints, though she couldn't point to any specific insult. My offense was simply to have told their story. I imagined them in the position of Nathan Zuckerman's brother Henry in *The Counterlife*. Reading his brother's books, Henry thinks, is like "having a very long argument with someone who wouldn't go away. . . . Nathan had got the monopoly on words, and the power and prestige that went with it."

With only a few weeks to go before publication, I sent a copy to Sally at Spring Lake Ranch, the therapeutic work community where she is currently living in the Green Mountains of Vermont. I had been putting this off. Sally had asked me to use her real name in the book, but that was without her knowing its contents. To harm her was the furthest thing from my mind, but in a way the very act of writing was a betrayal: I was exposing her psychosis, chronicling in detail what could have been painlessly left unsaid. "I've forgotten almost everything that happened that summer," she told me. "Some merciful manic amnesia, I guess." My descriptions of her—bristling uncontrollably, with her lips pressed fiercely together and her voice piercing me like a dart—were bound to throw her back to that awful time. At worst, it could trigger a fresh manic attack.

Before putting the book in the mail, I called Sally to let her know it was on the way. "You sound scared," she said. This usually meant that she was frightened as well.

I delivered the speech I had prepared: the memoir was a reconstruction of an event that took place twelve years ago; it wasn't a portrait of Sally as she was now. "Some of it may disturb you," I said.

My warning seemed to make her more eager to read it. She would get the book in time to finish it over the weekend. "I'll come up to the Ranch on Monday, so we can talk about it, if you feel you need to," I said. I also sent a copy to Bridget, her advisor and "team leader" at the Ranch.

On Sunday night Sally called me after finishing the book. "I felt I was reading about someone else, a fifteen-year-old girl named Sally who had been to hell and was the only one who didn't know it. How many people get to look at themselves in such a way?" After a brief telephone pause, she continued: "The cows escaped this morning. Everyone panicked: there goes half our meat for the winter! Luckily, we found them." She insisted that I drop my plans to visit her.

I was immensely relieved, but worried that she was acting too bright, too certain. I pictured her in the main house, with her unruly amber hair, looking out at the enormous vegetable garden, and the sloping hay fields beyond a stand of white birches. A Finnish immigrant, Wayne Sarcka, bought the land in 1932, with the idea of creating a utopian retreat for "the wounded and vulnerable." During the First World War, Sarcka had worked with British soldiers suffering from shell shock in Mesopotamia. The last time I visited, a few months ago, mud season was underway and my boots sank to the ankles in the melting snow. Sally was working on the maple-syrup crew, running sap through a series of tubes that looped from one maple tap to the next like a fence line. "People joke that they can't tell the residents from the staff," the crew director told me. "As far as we're concerned, there's no higher compliment."

When we spoke again the next day Sally was more critical. "You weren't fair to Mom. You made her out to be some kind of New Age flake." She added that her team leader, Bridget, didn't like my use of the term "crack-up." "She said she found it jarring. Harsh. It doesn't bother me. It's just that they talk differently here."

I'd heard this objection from others. An editor had complained that "crack-up" was "too old-fashioned, too F. Scott Fitzgerald." A writer who published a memoir about his own depression said that when he came across the term in the first paragraph of my book he lost all desire to read on. I tried to explain my attraction to "crack-up," with its suggestion of a psyche in fragments, of something whole that had come apart. I preferred it to "breakdown" which in some cases denoted nothing stronger than being reduced to tears. *Mental illness*, the term accepted as correct by almost everyone, covered every disorder in the American Psychiatric Association's *Diagnostic and Statistical Manual*, including premature ejaculation and cannabis-induced disorder.

I emailed Bridget, who wrote glowingly of Sally's progress at the Ranch. "She didn't take your book as hard as I was afraid she would. She says she wants more people here to read it. I don't think that's a good idea. She's feeling a bit like a celebrity. There's a danger that the image of the mentally ill Sally will overpower the image of health and wellness that she has worked hard to create and that she deserves to be able to project."

As for her distaste for "crack-up," Bridget wrote, "At first I thought, Oh boy, this is going to be a bumpy ride. But as I read further, I realized it was a form of self-flagellation: you were using it to beat yourself into an understanding of the change that had come over your daughter. Your memoir was just your way of exhaling."

When I reached Sally again, she said, "Forget about the book already. I told you I loved it. I've got to run. I'm late for work crew."

SINCE THE PUBLICATION OF MY BOOK a few weeks ago, the pattern of my days at the plywood desk in the corner of my bedroom on West 108th Street has changed. First, there is the writer's stock exchange, Amazon. It's not clear whether it's a wish for encouragement or self-torment that drives me to interrupt what I'm doing several times a day to check the book's sales ranking. Every hour the ranking is updated, a constantly fluctuating verdict from a vast open market of invisible traders, each pondering his personalized Amazon screen before clicking the "Add to Cart" option, passing over my book in favor of another. Even when your placing creeps up a few notches, you still feel like the insect in the movie *Antz* who complains of being the middle child in a family of a million.

Matters don't improve when customers who have bought the book take the trouble to post their opinions. "Acutely conscious pandering," reads the latest review of my account of my daughter's struggle with mental illness. "Don't waste your money," warns another. "I can overhear a story like this any day on the subway." One reader is put off by the way "the hapless narrator" allows himself to be "kicked around verbally by ascendant females, usually rendered in goddess-like imagery, not blatant but intended for subliminal imprint."

I am just beginning to wean myself from the Amazon habit when it is time to fly to the West Coast for a weeklong reading tour. First stop is Laguna in Southern California, where it takes me some minutes to realize I'm in a bookstore. The shelves are crammed with tote bags, calendars, greeting cards, stuffed animals, plastic snow globes, and Christmas candy, though it is still September. The events planner, a docile young woman with orange hair and a thick golden ring in her nose, takes me up to the second floor where the books are. "We were voted the best independent bookstore of 2008," she says, "because of all of the accessories we carry. It's a way to survive."

Five people show up for the reading, including an elderly woman who spends the entire time drinking from a Santa Claus mug (on sale downstairs), and reading a book called *Dewey* about a kitten who was dropped in the after-hours book return box of a small Iowa library, enriching the librarian's life.

My hotel is jarringly luxurious, replete with prowling call girls, extravagant floral bouquets, marble side tables, and vaguely recognizable celebrities climbing in and out of a parade of chauffeured cars. A woman with an Eva Peron hairdo hands me a flute of champagne and a certificate for a thirty-minute facial in the hotel spa. I count on one finger the number of books I sold in Laguna, and wonder how it matches up with the mounting expenses.

In my room next morning, I do a call-in radio interview with a rock-and-roll station that broadcasts out of the San Fernando Valley. "Let me try to get my head around this," says the host of the show, Tommy. "One day you wake up and your daughter is off the rails crazy? This is heavy stuff, dude. Tell us what happened." I'm laboring toward an explanation when Tommy snaps, "We'll have to leave it there," dumping me off the air with a barrage of advertisements for car tires, homeowner's credit, burial plots, and automobile insurance.

By late afternoon, I'm in San Francisco Bay on the island of Alameda, a funkily attractive place that claims to have given birth to the popsicle and Kewpie doll in the 1920s, when it served as a beach resort for day-trippers from San Francisco. It's the night of the first presidential debate, and to watch it I wander over to Alameda's Democratic Party headquarters, a narrow airless storefront off the main drag, packed with a raucous crowd. Palely projected onto a rumpled sheet that has been hung on the far wall, the debate has the feeling of a silent movie, with every utterance drowned out by a swell of hisses and cheers. I strike up a friendship with the man standing next to me, a tugboat captain, who announces to the assembled company in a booming voice that I'll be reading, after the debate, at the bookstore around the corner. I arrive there with dozens of Obamiacs in tow, aglow with their candidate's performance and eager, it seems, to hear my story.

The final stop is in Sonoma county, fifty miles north of San Francisco, winemaking country and the epicenter of the American Food Revolution—"locally grown produce, artistically prepared." For dinner: oysters on an unstable bed of parsnip-wasabi puree, with a side dish of dragon tongue bean succotash, to the accompaniment of piped-in "Zen" music. At

7:30 a.m., a horrifying hotel breakfast: butternut squash strata, with laura chenel chevre, currant beurre noisette, and glazed carrots. The waiter enumerates every condiment in the dish and commands me to enjoy.

The reading is at a handsome bookstore in Petaluma, "chicken capital of America," the landscape tawny and shaved. Afterward, a man with an Orson Welles voice and a Harvard education invites me to a bar across the street for a drink. He tells me that he writes a column on the "oracular arts" for a women's magazine in Japan. His chief interest is runes, an ancient Norse alphabet derived from rock carvings of the second Bronze Age and used as "a guide for shamans and tribal leaders throughout Europe."

He hands me a book he has written, a collection of "runic wisdom," one saying on each page, "a book of chance, like the I Ching, but with more emphasis on the spirit-life than on political success and power."

He flips the book open to a random page. "Feed your faith and you will be deeply nourished; feed your doubts and they will starve you." Then he tells me to pick a page, holding the little book in his palm, like a man presenting a card trick. I pick one and he reads it aloud, in a theatrical, suddenly brogue-inflected accent. "The winter of the spiritual life is upon you. You may find yourself entangled in a situation to whose implications you are, in effect, blind. You may feel powerless to do anything except submit, surrender, even sacrifice some long cherished desire."

My new friend pauses to let the significance of the oracle sink in, then asks what my ranking is on Amazon.

Sound Booth

I SPENT TWO-AND-A-HALF DAYS last week in a sound booth the size of a closet, recording an audio version of my book about my family's summer of madness. The night before I was to begin, the director called to warn me to wear clothes that wouldn't rustle, and to lay off coffee in the morning. "It may cause your tummy to rumble. The sound system has a way of picking up even the quietest extraneous noise." His voice was cultivated and tensely polite, his enunciation impressively clear, as if, in part, the call was intended to give me a pointer in good diction.

My main worry was the cough I couldn't get rid of. It shook me without warning into paroxysms that went on for a full minute or longer. If the rustling of cloth was disruptive, what would be the effect of those dry bronchial barks? I decided to come armed with a bottle of codeine-laced syrup, like a wino with his muscatel, just in case.

At the studio I was met by a short, vigorous broad-chested man of about sixty: David Rapkin, the director with whom I had spoken on the phone. He explained to me that the goal was "to make the listener feel present with the meaning of the words, so that he has a transparent relationship with the text. He forgets that he is listening and simply experiences the story." I noted the subtle theatricality of his delivery, musical and stentorian at the same time. He should be the one recording my book, I thought.

He had carefully prepared for the session, reading the book twice, compiling a list of characters, a timeline and a breakdown of major scenes. Referring to my daughter, he said: "When Sally speaks, I think it would be a mistake to view her through any lens other than her own."

It occurred to me that for the moment he was more connected to the material than I was. My impulse was to forget it. I had tried to plough through the book again last night, but had stopped cold after a couple of pages. Reciting it off the cuff, I hoped, would allow me to inject it with a spontaneity that countless drafts and the tedium of copyediting had hammered out of me.

I took my place in the sound booth and peered out at David and the young sound engineer on the other side of the glass. I imagined myself as their antagonist, the obstacle standing in the way of the smooth completion of a job like hundreds of others they had performed. On cue, I started reading, in the reluctant voice of a man embarking on an unachievable task. David seemed explosive from this vantage point, hunched over the text, monitoring my every word, making sure I didn't stray "off book," policing my breath, my popped "p's," my persuasiveness, my fluency.

Hearing the thickness in my voice, he fed me a powerful throat lozenge called VocalZones, favored by opera singers, and available, he claimed, at only one pharmacy in Manhattan. "It's like getting hit in the head with an iceberg," he said.

A few pages later my stomach began to rumble, which in the foam-walled booth sounded as loud as thunder. Ignoring David's warning, I had drunk two cups of coffee before leaving my apartment. He motioned me out of the booth and handed me a banana. "Eat it slowly."

It took care of the rumble, but soon he interrupted me again. I was sounding "gluey." This time he produced a green apple from his bag. "Take five or six bites. Chew as much as you can. It's the only remedy."

My cough erupted and I surreptitiously took a swig of the codeine syrup.

This was a mistake. The words began to reconfigure themselves on the page, like information on a train station time board. My New York accent grew heavier. It was as if I was feeling my way through a foreign language, mangling words, running out of steam halfway through a sentence, unnerved by the chasm between the way I heard language in my head and the objective auditory reality that reached David's ears on the other side of the glass. I was unable to say "accompanying" no matter how many times I tried, and after ten takes, stammering and flustered, I simply changed it to "escorting."

"Manage your breath," said David. "Slow down. And don't worry, when it comes to pronunciation I'm like a dog with a bone."

By late afternoon I was automatically offering a second take to every sentence, with a slightly different inflection, giving the editors an alternative draft to choose from later.

"Stop directing yourself. It's destructive to the process," said David angrily. And our first session came to an end.

It turned out that we lived in the same neighborhood, and we agreed to share a cab uptown. In response to my anxious questions, David assured me that the day's work had gone "just fine." I recognized in him the particular sophistication of Manhattanites who came of age in the 1940s and early 1950s: a clashing sense of the arcane, the absurd, the anarchic, and an inherited immigrant's severity. He began producing audiobooks in the 1980s, shortly after the Norelco cassette recorder made the product a viable business. "My first was Elmore Leonard's *Glitz*, in 1985. One of the best dialogue writers of his time." He took pride in his ear for dialect and accents, his sensitivity to verbal ticks and unconscious speech patterns. He had discovered several such patterns in me, correcting them each time in the same patient, neutral tone.

The cab let us off on Broadway and David went into a deli for a pack of cigarettes. Two men behind the counter were talking in a strange language. After listening attentively, David guessed they were speaking Pashto, earning a round of delighted handshakes and several extra books of matches.

The following day he coached me in giving each of my characters his own verbal stamp, in one case feeding me a flawless German accent phrase by phrase. After we finished recording, he confided to me that he suffered from a powerful urge to pun, and had had to struggle to restrain himself from doing so, because "it was antisocial, it played with people's minds, forcing them into a word consciousness that made the flow of conversation impossible." It was the price of his intense pleasure in the sound of words.

I remarked that this kind of verbal facility was linked to certain forms of psychosis. "I know," he said. "My sister was schizophrenic. It's partly why I wanted to work on your book." Then he repeated what I had often told myself while writing the memoir: "All I wanted was for you to get out of the way so the story could tell itself."

IN ELEMENTARY SCHOOL I had an ultra-Orthodox teacher who objected to our taking art class, because it broke God's second commandment: "Thou shalt not make unto thee any graven image or any likeness of any thing that is in heaven above or that is in the earth beneath or that is in the water under the earth." It referred to the Ancient Egyptian practice of praying to statues; it was a political edict that had lost its relevance the day the Romans closed the last Egyptian temples seventeen hundred years ago. The teacher told us that the commandment was a spiritual protection against the danger of seeing what might come before your eyes. The picture of a living creature was a form of soul theft.

Lately I've been thinking that in a way my teacher was right—not in the sense of making pictures, but about writing of people you know. Most people are disturbed when an experience they've had is told for them—and the closer the person is to you, the more he or she is apt to feel wronged. What captures their attention is not the scrupulous portrait you've drawn, but rather the unpleasantness of seeing themselves as a manipulated object in the drama of their own life. "You've no idea who I am," was my brother's response to a story of mine in which he appeared. Referring to a different piece, another family member said, "It's a false me acting like me. I wish you'd stop this kind of writing." A couple of years ago, I staked out a relative's apartment so I could intercept from the mailman a magazine with a story I'd written about him. When my wife appears in a piece, I do my best to keep it from her eyes.

I have been avoiding Eric, my high school friend and former landlord, since the publication last September of my memoir about my daughter's breakdown. Eric is a minor character in the book. We were living at the time in a building he owned on Bank Street in Greenwich Village. In the memoir, as in life, he is writing a novel that I believe he has no intention of finishing. Every year, under the guise of revising it, he retypes the manuscript and gives it to me to read. The rent I'm paying is affordable, but subject to Eric's whim, and partly in order to protect my position in the building, I play along, discussing the novel with him in such a way as to make it seem viable and alive.

Finding myself in the West Village last week, I neglected to make my usual detour around Bank Street, and walked past the building. "Hey, what you doing here, man. You come to make trouble? To make people upset?" It was Marcus, the Jamaican plumber who ran a business on the ground floor and slept in a small apartment in the basement. We had always been friendly, linked by our dependence on Eric's generosity and the small favors done for him in return. "You a big shot now? You a rich man?" He offered me his hand to slap with its missing fourth finger—an accident with a boiler. "Everyone got to give some blood," he said at the time. We remembered the tenant he gave a rose to the day she moved into the building. "She still lives here, and you know what, she never thanked me for that flower. She never thanked me for nothing." I wanted to know who was in my old apartment, a glowing, decrepit tenement palace, with seventeen windows on the top floor. Marcus made it clear I didn't deserve such information. "Why you never come around?" I asked him if Eric was about. "I haven't seen him."

I entered the building and began climbing the stairs. It was wonderfully unchanged, with its Moroccan-blue doors, landings crowded with pictures and masks, and remnants of various projects to improve the building—a gallon of paint, a bucket of plaster—that had been abandoned, like Eric's novel. I made it to the roof, sixty feet above the street, where I used to sleep during the hottest summer nights, when the air conditioner's fuse would burn out. Sometimes I was joined by a drunk named Ritchie who mopped the building for Eric and liked to crash there too, another beneficiary of Eric's largesse. I remembered being impressed when Eric kept Ritchie on after he stole one tenant's bicycle and ran off with another's shoes. Returning to the apartment in the morning, I might find Eric on a visit, snoring on the foldout couch or making himself breakfast.

About an hour after I left the building, Eric sat down next to me on the platform of the Fourteenth Street subway station where I was waiting to take the number 1 train uptown. He wore a baggy brown corduroy jacket and was holding an acoustic guitar with two strings missing, as if it was something he had just found. He waited for me to say hello first, with his sly, embarrassed smile. I wondered if he was going to slug me. But all we did was talk like two people mimicking friendship, trying to remember what we used to talk about before. Neither mentioned the book, though I knew that he had read it—a mutual friend had told me it had "stabbed" him. "He had no idea you'd been humoring him all those years. He was crushed. You didn't have to write it that way. It's not the kind of news about yourself you want people to hear." I would have liked to apologize, but it wouldn't have been sincere. "I've been thinking about you," I said. "Me too."

When the train arrived, he left the guitar on the bench and walked up the stairs and out of the station. He had probably spotted me on the street and followed me down for the sole purpose of having the encounter. It couldn't have satisfied him. Several readers had assured me that my portrayal of Eric was sympathetic—"written with real fondness," one said. I knew this wasn't altogether true, and that it made it worse for Eric that it seemed to be so. "You didn't betray a secret," said the reader. "You didn't make anything up. So where's the problem?" Eric had once commented on how closely I listened to him. Enough to steal a piece of his soul.

The Antidote to Dread

I HAVE BEEN THINKING about the zombie effect of watching television, the satisfying passivity it causes after forty-five minutes or an hour of continuous exposure, the limp body and glazed-over eyes. The side effects resemble those of certain psychiatric drugs, when the imbiber falls under a peculiar spell of indifference, and the world looks as if it is being seen through the wrong end of a telescope. There's action enough, but it flows in one direction—toward you—as you lie in a state of reasonably contented inertia. What you are under the influence of is "the antidote to existential dread," as Don DeLillo called it, whether you are watching *Teletubbies* or another episode of humanity's sorrow.

A few days ago, the drug was withdrawn. My television reception was cut off. Without warning, the soothing pictures that usually emanate from the screen became a thick black-and-white blizzard with a soundtrack like high-speed traffic.

It was reminiscent of when the transmitter on top of the World Trade Center's north tower was knocked out on 9/11. One channel only projected a message. It came from the cable service company inviting me to pay for "the programming" that, by some regrettable oversight, I had been "enjoying free of cost" for the past eight years.

My wife, Pat, who rarely watched television, was delighted. "Let's leave it unplugged." Unsympathetic to my feeling of deprivation, she cited a recommendation by psychologists that children under the age of two avoid exposure to television in any form. It reminded me of the warning about feeding tuna to children because of the risk of mercury poisoning. Both cause developmental impairment. "Face it, Michael, it can't be very good for a man in his fifties either." Our ten-year-old son didn't appear to notice what we had lost. He was busy exercising his thumbs on a hand-held gaming device with insertable mint-sized disks, each with its own circuit board designed to launch him on a fresh adventure.

Technically, I still had television: the set was sitting where it had always been, ready to receive rented DVDs. But movies have a purposeful aura that is different from the trivial perpetuity of live air-time being filled. Part of television's appeal is that it exists without interruption, it is deathless and unimportant, it brings its measure of eternity into the apartment.

The wee hours of the morning are when I rely on television, and yesterday after midnight I found myself reaching for the remote control before remembering there would be nothing to watch and I would have to face the stimulation of insomnia without assistance. A book is of little use under the circumstances, since reading usually makes me feel more awake than before.

I described my withdrawal symptoms to a friend who immediately became panicked on my behalf. "What are you going to do? You're wired for TV." He is a writer who lives alone and is also dependent at certain hours on the screen's benign companionship. With approval, he quoted Marshall McLuhan (who for his part had been paraphrasing the novelist Max Frisch): "Technology arranges the world so we don't have to experience it."

All of technology, in this view, is an extension of the human body. "Electronic circuitry, for example, is the nervous system reaching outward," said my friend. He regarded our desire to shield ourselves from experience as a logical response to our insecurities, a natural expression of who we are. He quoted another of McLuhan's dicta: "We shape our tools and then our tools shape us." So you see, he said, "it's like when the electricity goes out. You're not set up to live without it, and there's no use fooling yourself into believing it would be a virtue to try to do so. Now call the cable company and get yourself plugged in, because, believe me, man, you need the protection."

Another, younger, friend congratulated me for having become "a twenty-first century man." Apparently, the decline of television viewership began to alarm network executives in the spring of 2003 when 20 percent fewer men between the ages of eighteen and twenty-four were tuning in during prime time than in the spring of the year before. "We let them get out of the habit of watching television," said David Poltrack, chief researcher for CBS. "Now I don't know how we're going to get them back in front of their sets."

At first the decline was thought to be the fault of video games, and recording devices that allowed viewers to fashion their own TV schedules, and, improbably, the deployment of increasing numbers of young men to Afghanistan and Iraq. But as the trend continued it became clear that the Internet, the usual destroyer of thriving businesses, was to blame. People were getting highlights of their favorite shows from You Tube. It seemed to be enough for them. There were other things to occupy their attention online. "Welcome to the age of the three-minute sketch," my younger friend said.

For the effective treatment of insomnia, however, the minimum dose of television time is one hour. It was McLuhan's idea that every era creates a utopian image of itself, "a nostalgic, rear-view mirror image" that puts it out of touch with the present that is eternally disappointing. Mine was for the "decency standard" that program executives chafed at in the 1960s, the three lone channels, the bomb shelter alerts, and movies such as *Robin Hood* and *The Hunchback of Notre Dame* playing in a continuous loop on Sundays. To recapture the feeling, I had taken to turning on the set and accepting whatever happened to appear on the screen. It could be an infomercial about skin cream or an evangelical preacher or a congressman addressing an empty chamber on Capitol Hill, as was often the case at three in the morning.

I didn't care. The point was to be watching television; the content was of little importance. I couldn't look elsewhere when it was on, it was like staring into a fire. "What further argument do you need to keep it unplugged?" Pat asked when I told her I was planning to have the cable company reinstate our service.

I had no answer. Maybe I just missed the emptiness, and didn't know where else to find it.

My Grandfather's Watch

MY MATERNAL GRANDFATHER'S POCKET WATCH has reappeared behind a drawer stuffed with old photographs and letters. I had mourned its loss after moving apartments ten years ago. His name—Jacob Kurnick—is engraved on the back, making it, as far as I know, one of only three pieces of material evidence that he existed. Embossed on the cover is a greyhound with a diamond-studded walking stick in its mouth—a foppish touch and completely at odds with the official family image of him as a selfless doctor who would go hungry before billing his needy patients.

"He'd give you the shirt off his back," my mother said. "Even if it was custom made."

Jacob died in 1935 when my mother was thirteen, and the mention of his name still provokes a hushed reverence. I continue to picture him through the ache of my mother's memory, our family saint, surrounded by a halo of Mittel-European brilliance and good deeds.

Exhibit number two of Jacob's life is the menu from the first-class cabin of a German ocean liner that—I had somehow got it in my head to believe—had carried him across the Atlantic in 1908 when he emigrated to New York. The menu was proof of Jacob's distinction, and as a boy I would ask my mother to show it to me, a cherished item with silver script lettering that made it look like a wedding invitation. He was, I later believed, my tenuous link to the Europe of Kafka and Joseph Roth. If only he had lived.

He was the opposite of my other grandfather, Louie, with his welding torch and illiteracy, who sweated it out until the mid-1960s. Louie came, in Roth's words, from "a strange and mournful ghetto world," where thousands of "Eastern grotesques" were "welded together . . . like a landslip of unhappiness and grime."

In the early 1920s, Jacob made a fortune investing his earnings as a doctor in a cousin's mayonnaise factory. This must have been when he acquired his pocket watch and tailor-made clothes. My mother remembers insisting that the family chauffeur let her off two blocks from school. "I couldn't bear to be seen climbing out of that enormous car. I knew my classmates would hate me."

At this point, the story took on the aura of a folk tale, in which each piece of good fortune is methodically withdrawn. Jacob was infected with a rare blood disease, called pemphigus vulgaris, which he diagnosed himself, hiding it from his family until he had to take to his bed, tended by his daughter. After his death, the mayonnaise cousin cheated them out of their money. Seen from the point of view of my mother as a grieving young girl, the details of those events seemed strangely unreal. Suddenly she was living with my grandmother in a tiny apartment in Brooklyn, without a breadwinner, in the middle of the Great Depression.

"You'll understand me when I tell you that if Jacob hadn't died I would never have met your father. We traveled in different circles. I would have been more likely to marry a doctor."

Death intensified Jacob, and to my father, who had dropped out of school, he was an unvanquishable rival. My mother invoked him, I thought, to carve out an area of superiority with my father, who otherwise seemed to hold the upper hand. It was as if her life with him, with us, was her substitute life. The subtle air of compromise that she projected, of having settled for less than she was born to have, silenced and enraged him.

Hanukkah at my mother's apartment: a blazing menorah in one corner, an arrangement of pine twigs in another. "A little something for all of us pagans," she says. Frail after a recent stay in the hospital, she sits on the couch greeting her various sons and daughters-in-law, while her second husband protectively caresses her hand. She wears a green tuxedo-like suit, and a glowing face, and we marvel at her. I am reminded of the fashion show she put on twelve years ago, when my father was a terminal case on the cancer ward. Each morning she'd arrive in a fresh outfit, stretching her wardrobe to the limit, not a hair out of place during that entire sweltering July. The nurses delighted in her efforts, and so did my father. "You look like you've come to pick up an award," he told her. Her bright, careful veneer calmed him, I thought. She had become her own impeccable ideal.

In its familiar place on the wall hangs the photograph of Jacob, exhibit three: a dour round-faced thickly moustachioed man in a brown suit, his cheeks rouged by the studio photographer's airbrush. Rather than sharpen the reality of his existence, the picture, with its painted sky-blue backdrop, seems to belong more than ever to an imaginary past.

At my request, my mother takes out the transatlantic ocean-liner menu. I haven't seen it since I was a teenager, and now note that it is not from a German ship, as I had supposed, but from the *President Harding* of the United States Lines, which traveled from Manhattan to Hamburg.

The year on the menu is 1926, when Jacob was thirty-four. "We were on our way to Heidelberg, where my father was to spend a year at the medical school, doing postgraduate work in his specialty, ENT. I was four years old." The offhand precision with which my mother speaks of the trip surprises me. I wonder if she had always told it this way, and if I had been the one to hear it the way I wanted to, embellishing my connection to the past.

I ask her when Jacob first came to America.

"When he was fifteen, the same age Louie was when he arrived. They were both from Russia, though they didn't know each other, of course."

Hadn't she implied something different about him?

She smiles mutely.

Why did I think he was German?

"I can't help you with that, Michael."

A native New Yorker, Michael Greenberg is
the author of the memoir *Hurry Down Sunshine*
(Other Press, 2008), published in sixteen
countries and chosen as one of the best books
of 2008 by *Time*, the *San Francisco Chronicle*,
Amazon.com, and *Library Journal*. He is a
columnist for the *Times Literary Supplement*.
His writing has been published in such varied
places as *O, The Oprah Magazine* and *The New
York Review of Books*. He lives in New York.

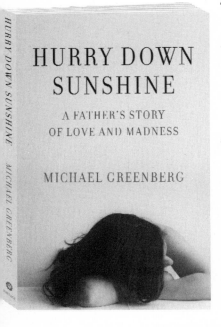